Uruguay

Ben Box

D0812879

Credits

Footprint credits
Editor: Alan Murphy
Production and layout: Emma Bryers,
Elysia Alim, Danielle Bricker
Maps: Kevin Feeney

Managing Director: Andy Riddle
Commercial Director: Patrick Dawson
Publisher: Alan Murphy
Publishing Managers: Felicity Laughton,
Nicola Gibbs
Digital Editors: Jo Williams, Tom Mellors
Marketing and PR: Liz Harper
Sales: Diane McEntee
Advertising: Renu Sibal
Finance and Administration: Elizabeth
Taylor

Photography credits
Front cover: Kobby Dagan / Shutterstock
Back cover: Galina Barskaya / Shutterstock

Printed in Great Britain by CPI Antony Rowe,
Chippenham, Wiltshire

MIX
Paper from
responsible sources
FSC® C013604
www.fsc.org

Every effort has been made to ensure that
the facts in this guidebook are accurate.
However, travellers should still obtain
advice from consulates, airlines, etc, about
travel and visa requirements before travelling.
The authors and publishers cannot accept
responsibility for any loss, injury or
inconvenience however caused.

Publishing information
Footprint *Focus Uruguay*
1st edition
© Footprint Handbooks Ltd
September 2011

ISBN: 978 1 908206 28 2
CIP DATA: A catalogue record for this book
is available from the British Library

® Footprint Handbooks and the
Footprint mark are a registered
trademark of Footprint Handbooks Ltd

Published by Footprint
6 Riverside Court
Lower Bristol Road
Bath BA2 3DZ, UK
T +44 (0)1225 469141
F +44 (0)1225 469461
www.footprinttravelguides.com

Distributed in the USA by Globe Pequot Press,
Guilford, Connecticut

The content of Footprint *Focus Uruguay*
has been taken directly from Footprint's
South American Handbook, which was
researched and written by Ben Box.

Contents

ARGENTINA

BRAZIL

Bella Unión   Río Quaraí   Artigas

Termas del Arapey

Rivera

Salto

Termas de Daymán   Minas de Corrales

Termas de Guaviyú   Tacuarembó   Aceguá

Paysandú   Guichón   Tambores   Ansina   Melo

Curtina   Las Toscas

Paso de los Toros   Rincón del Bonete (Lago Artificial)

Tres Bocas   Río Negro   Quebrada de los Cuervos

Fray Bentos   Mercedes   Carlos Reyes

Soriano   Cerro Chato   Treinta y Tres

Palmitas   Durazno   Sarandí del Yí   José R Varela

Trinidad   Pirajá   Lascano

Dolores   Sarandí Grande

Nueva Palmira   Cardona   Florida   Cerro Colorado   Velásquez

Calera de las Huérfanas   Nueva Helvecia   San José de Mayo   Aiguá   Castillo

Carmelo   Rosario   Colonia Valdense   Canelones   Minas   San Carlos

Conchillas   Sta Rosa   Solís   La Paloma

Colonia del Sacramento   Libertad

Río de la Plata   Atlántida

MONTEVIDEO   Piriápolis   Maldonado

Punta del Este

Atlantic Ocean

N

20 km
20 miles

4 ● Uruguay

Uruguay is a land of rolling hills, best explored on horseback, or by staying at the many estancias that have opened their doors to visitors. It also has its feet in the Atlantic Ocean and one of the best ways to arrive is by ferry across the shipping lanes of the Río de la Plata. Montevideo, the capital and main port, is refurbishing its historical centre to match the smart seaside neighbourhoods, but its atmosphere is far removed from the cattle ranches of the interior.

West of Montevideo is Colonia del Sacramento, a former smuggling town turned gambling centre, and a colonial gem where race horses take their exercise in the sea. Up the Río Uruguay there are pleasant towns, some with bridges to Argentina, some with thermal springs. Also by the river is Fray Bentos, a town that lent its name to corned beef for generations, which is now an industrial museum.

Each summer, millions of holidaymakers flock to Punta del Este, one of the most famous resorts on the continent, but if crowds are not your cup of *mate* (the universal beverage), go out of season. Alternatively, venture up the Atlantic coast towards Brazil for empty beaches and fishing villages, sea lions, penguins and the occasional old fortress. And anywhere you go, take your binoculars because the birdwatching is excellent.

Planning your trip

Where to go

Montevideo, the capital, is the business heart of the country and has an interesting Ciudad Vieja (old city). The highlights are Mercado del Puerto, the former dockside market, which has become an emporium for traditional food and drink, and the magnificently restored Teatro Solís and the pedestrian Calle Sarandí. Within the city's limits are a number of beaches, which continue along the north shore of the Río de la Plata and on to the Atlantic seaboard. The most famous resort is **Punta del Este** which, in season (December-February), is packed with Argentines, Brazilians and locals taking their summer break. Beyond Punta del Este, there are quieter beaches with less infrastructure, but with sand dunes and other natural features. Along the coast, impressive villas and condominiums blend with their surroundings, a sort of museum of contemporary South American architecture under the open sky.

West of the capital is **Colonia del Sacramento**, a unique remnant of colonial building in this part of the continent. It is well preserved, standing on a small peninsula, and has one of the principal ferry ports for passenger traffic from Buenos Aires. Consequently it is a popular but costly place, but well worth a visit. Continuing west you come to the confluence of the Río Uruguay with the Plata estuary. Up river are the last vestiges of the meat canning industry at **Fray Bentos**, which has a museum commemorating what used to be one of Uruguay's main businesses. Further upstream are towns such as **Paysandú** and the historic **Salto**, from which you can cross to Argentina, and the hot springs which have been developed into resorts.

The centre of the country is mainly agricultural land, used for livestock and crops. Many *estancias* (farms) accept visitors. Daytrips out of Montevideo, Punta del Este, or Colonia, for instance, to an *estancia*, usually involve a meal, handicraft shopping and an educational element. Those ranches which offer lodging let you take part in the daily tasks, as these are working farms; you can do as much or as little as you like. Horse riding is the main activity and is suitable for all.

When to go

The climate is temperate, often windy, with summer heat tempered by Atlantic breezes. Winter (June-September) is damp; temperatures average 10-16°C, but can sometimes fall to freezing. Summer (December-March) temperatures average 21-27°C. There is always some wind and the nights are relatively cool. The rainfall, with prolonged wet periods in July/August, averages about 1,200 mm at Montevideo and some 250 more in the north, but the amount varies yearly.

Most tourists visit during the summer, which is also high season, when prices rise and hotels and transport need advance bookings. Seasonal variations for Montevideo and Punta del Este are given on pages 20 and 46. In the low season on the coast many places close.

Don't miss ...

Numbers refer to the map on page 4.

Getting there

Air

Most South American countries have direct flights from **Europe**; only Paraguay does not. In many cases, though, the choice of departure point is limited to Madrid and one or two other cities (Paris or Amsterdam, for instance). Argentina, Brazil and Venezuela have the most options: France, Germany, Italy, Spain and the UK (although the last named not to Venezuela). Brazil also has flights from Lisbon to a number of cities. Where there are no direct flights connections can be made in the USA (Miami, or other gateways), Buenos Aires, Rio de Janeiro or São Paulo. **Main US gateways** are Miami, Houston, Dallas, Atlanta and New York. On the west coast, Los Angeles has flights to several South American cities. If buying airline tickets routed through the USA, check that US taxes are included in the price. Flights from **Canada** are mostly via the USA, although there are direct flights from Toronto to Bogotá and Santiago. Likewise, flights from **Australia** and **New Zealand** are best through Los Angeles, except for the Qantas/LAN route from Sydney and Auckland to Santiago, and Qantas' route to Buenos Aires. From **Japan** and from **South Africa** there are direct flights to Brazil. Within **Latin America** there is plenty of choice on local carriers and some connections on US or European airlines. For airpasses, see below. To Guyana, the main routes are via the Caribbean (Port of Spain, Trinidad and Barbados) or New York, Miami and Toronto. Suriname is served by flights from Amsterdam and Port of Spain, while Guyane has flights from Paris and the French-speaking Caribbean. All three have air connections with northern Brazil.

Prices and discounts

Most airlines offer discounted fares on scheduled flights through agencies who specialize in this type of fare. For a list of these agencies see page . If you buy discounted air tickets always check the reservation with the airline concerned to make sure the flight still exists. Also remember the IATA airlines' schedules change in March and October each year, so if you're going to be away a long time it's best to leave return flight coupons open. Peak times are 7 December-15 January and 10 July-10 September. If you intend travelling during those times, book as far ahead as possible. Between February and May and September and November special offers may be available.

Getting around

Flight connections If flying from Uruguay to make an international connection in Buenos Aires, make sure your flight goes to Ezeiza International Airport (eg American Airlines or TAM), not Aeroparque (almost all Aerolíneas Argentinas or Pluna flights). Luggage is not transferred automatically to Ezeiza and you will have to travel one hour between the airports by taxi or bus. If you need a visa to enter Argentina, you must get a transit visa (takes up to four weeks to process in Montevideo), just to transfer between airports. See also Tax for airport taxes, page 11.

Bus and road All main cities and towns are served by good companies originating from the Tres Cruces Terminal in Montevideo (www.trescruces.com.uy, for schedules and fares, but purchase must be made in person and early if travelling to popular destinations at peak holiday time). There are good services to neighbouring countries. Details are given in the text. Driving your own or a rented vehicle (see page 29) is a viable way to explore Uruguay, as it allows flexibility and access to further destinations. **Hitching** is not easy.

Train The passenger services are slow commuter services from Montevideo to Progreso, Canelones, Santa Lucía, 25 de Agosto and San José de Mayo; and from Montevideo to Pando and Sudriers.

Maps Automóvil Club del Uruguay, publishes road maps of the city and country, as do **Esso** and **Ancap**. A good road map of Uruguay and Montevideo (all in one) is published by **Silveira Mapas**, *Mapa de la República Oriental del Uruguay/Plano de la capital Montevideo*, US$6.50. ITM of Vancouver also publish a country map (1:800,000). Official maps are issued by **Instituto Geográfico Militar**, Abreu y 8 de Octubre, T487 1810.

Sleeping

Camping There are lots of sites. Most towns have municipal sites (quality varies). Many sites along the Ruta Interbalnearia, but most of these close off season. The Tourist Office in Montevideo issues a good guide to campsites and youth hostels; see references in main text. The annual Guía de Verano is good for sites and prices, particularly at the beach resorts.

Youth hostels Many good quality hostels can be found in Montevideo and other cities and towns (see recommendations in Sleeping sections). **Hostelling International** ① *Paraguay 1212 (y Canelones), Montevideo, T900 5749, www.hosteluruguay.org*, has 20 member hostels.

Eating and drinking

Eating out Dinner hours are generally 2000-0100. Restaurants usually charge *cubierto* (bread and place setting), costing US$1-3, and more in Punta del Este. Lunch is generally served from 1300-1500, when service often stops until dinner. A *confitería* is an informal place which serves meals at any time, as opposed to a *restaurante*, which serves meals at set times. Uruguay does not have a great selection of international restaurants.

Sleeping and eating price codes

Sleeping

$$$$	over US$150	**$$$**	US$66-150
$$	US$30-65	**$**	under US$30

Price codes refer to the cost of two people sharing a double room in the high season.

Eating

$$$	over US$12	**$$**	US$6-12	**$**	under US$6

Prices refer to the average cost of a two-course meal for one person, not including drinks or service charge.

Vegetarians may have to stick to salads or pasta, as even the dishes which are "meatless" are served with ham or bacon.

Food In general, you have two choices: meat or Italian food. Beef is eaten at almost all meals. Most restaurants are *parrilladas* (grills) where the main cuts are *asado* (ribs); *pulpa* (no bones), *lomo* (fillet steak) and entrecote. Steak prices normally indicate the quality of the cut. Also very popular are *chorizos* and *salchichas*, both types of sausage. More exotic Uruguayan favorites include *morcilla* (blood sausage, salty or sweet), *chinchulines* or *chotos* (small or large intestines), *riñones* (kidneys) and *molleja* (sweetbreads). *Cordero* (lamb) and *brochettes* (skewers/kebabs) are also common. Grilled *provolone*, *morrones* (red peppers), *boniatos* (sweet potatos), and *chimichurri* sauce are also omnipresent. *Chivitos* (large, fully loaded steak burgers) and *milanesa* (fried breaded chicken or beef) are also popular; usually eaten with mixed salad (lettuce, tomato, onion), or chips. All Italian dishes are delicious, from bread to pastas to raviolis to desserts. Pizza is very common and good. Seafood includes squid, mussels, shrimp, salmon, and *lenguado* (sole). For snacks, *medialunas* (croissants) are often filled with ham and/or cheese, either hot or cold; toasted sandwiches and quiche are readily available; *panchos* are hot dogs; *picada* (crackers or breads, cheese, olives, coldcuts) is a common afternoon favourite. Desserts, mostly of Italian origin, are excellent. *Dulce de leche* (similar to caramel) and *dulce de membrillo* (quince cheese) are ubiquitous ingredients. As in Argentina, *alfajores* are a favourite sweet snack. Ice cream is excellent everywhere.

Drink The beers are good (**Patricia** has been recommended). Local wines vary, but tannat is the regional speciality (eg **Don Pascual, Pisano**). See www.vino-uruguay.com and www.uruguay winetours.com. Whisky is the favourite spirit in Uruguay, normally Johnny Walker. The local spirits include *uvita*, *caña* and *grappamiel* (honey liquor). In the Mercado del Puerto, Montevideo, a *medio medio* is half still white wine, half sparkling white (elsewhere a *medio medio* is half *caña* and half whisky). *Espillinar* is a cross between whisky and rum. Try the *clérico*, a mixture of wine and fruit juices. Very good fresh fruit juices and mineral water are common. *Mate* is the drink of choice between meal hours. Coffee is good, normally served espresso-style after a meal. Milk, sold in plastic containers, is excellent, skimmed to whole (*descremada* to *entera*)

Essentials A-Z

Accident and emergency
Emergency T911. Ambulance T105 or 911.
Fire service T104. Road police T108. Tourist
Police in Montevideo, at Colonia y Av del
Libertador, T0800-8226.

Electricity
220 volts 50 cycles AC. Various plugs used:
round 2-pin or flat 2-pin (most common),
oblique 2-pin with earth, 3 round pins in a line.

Embassies and consulates
Visit www.embassy.goabroad.com for a
complete list.

Festivals and events
Public holidays 1 Jan, 6 Jan; Carnival;
Easter week; 19 Apr; 1 and 18 May, 19 Jun;
18 Jul; 25 Aug (the night before is **Noche de
la Nostalgia**, when people gather in *boliches*
to dance to old songs); 12 Oct; 2 Nov; 25 Dec.

Carnival begins in late Jan/early Feb and
lasts for some 40 days until Carnival week,
officially Mon and Tue before Ash Wed
(many firms close for the whole week). The
most prominent elements in Carnival are
Candombe, representing the rituals of the
African slaves brought to the Río de la Plata
in colonial times through drumming and
dance. The complex polyrhythms produced
by the mass of drummers advancing down
the street in the 'Llamadas' parades is very
impressive. The other main element is
Murga, a form of street theatre withparody,
satire, singing and dancing by elaboately
made-up and costumed performers.

Business also comes to a standstill during
Holy Week, which coincides with La
Semana Criolla (horse-breaking, stunt riding
by cowboys, dances and song). Department
stores close only from Good Fri. Banks and
offices close Thu-Sun. Easter Mon is not a
holiday. A weekend of Sep or Oct is chosen

annually for celebrating the **Día del
Patrimonio** (Heritage Day) throughout the
country: hundreds of buildings, both public
or private, including embassies, are open to
the public for that day only. Also special
train services run. Mid-Dec there is a
Fireworks night at Pocitos beach.

Money → *US$1=18.30, €1=26.25 (Aug 2011).*
The currency is the *peso uruguayo*. Bank
notes:5, 10, 20, 50, 100, 200, 500, 1,000 and
2,000 pesos uruguayos. Coins: 50 centésimos,
1, 2, 5 and 10 pesos. Any amount of currency
can be taken in or out. Rates change often.

There's no restriction on foreign exchange
transactions (so it is a good place to stock
up with US$ bills, though AmEx and some
banks refuse to do this for credit cards;
most places charge 3% commission for
such transactions). Those banks that give
US$ cash against a credit card are given
in the text. Most ATMs in Montevideo can
dispense both Uruguayan pesos and US$.
Dollars cash can be purchased when leaving
the country. Changing Argentine pesos into
Uruguayan pesos is usually a marginally
worse rate than for dollars. Brazilian *reais*
get a much worse rate. US$ notes are
accepted for some services, including
most hotels and some restaurants.

Cost of travelling Prices vary considerably
between summer and winter in tourist
destinations, Punta del Este being one of
the most expensive summer resort in Latin
America. In Montevideo, allow US$60 daily
for a cheap hotel, eating the *menú del día*
and travelling by bus. Internet price varies
around US$0.70 to US$2 per hr.

Credit cards In some places there is a
10% charge to use Visa and MasterCard.
Most banks operate with **Banred** ATMs for
Visa or MasterCard withdrawals. MasterCard
emergency line call collect to USA,

T1-636-722 7111, or 02-902 5555. Visa
emergency line, call collect T00-044-20-
7937 8091. Most cheaper hotels outside
major cities do not accept credit cards.

Safety
Personal security offers few problems in
most of Uruguay. Petty theft does occur in
Montevideo, most likely in tourist areas or
markets. Beggars are often seen trying to
sell small items or simply asking for money.
They are not dangerous. The Policía Turística
patrol the streets of the capital.

Tax
Airport tax US$17 on all air travellers
leaving Uruguay for Buenos Aires,
Aeroparque, but US$31 to Ezeiza and
all other countries (payable in US$,
local currency or by credit card),
and a tax of 3% on all tickets issued
and paid for in Uruguay.
VAT/IVA 22%, 10% on certain basic items.

Telephone → *Country code +598.*
Road information: T1954. Ringing: long equal
tones, long pauses. Engaged: short tones,
short pauses. Mobile phone numbers are
prefixed by 098, 099.

Time
GMT -3 (Sep-Mar -2).

Tipping
Restaurant and cafés usually include service,
but an additional 10% is expected. Porters
at the airport: US$1 per piece of luggage.
Taxis: 5-10% of fare.

Tourist information
Ministry of Tourism Edif Depósito Santos,
Rambla 25 de Agosto y Yacaré, T02-188 5100,
www.turismo.gub.uy and www.uruguay
natural.com. It has information on birdwatching and the best places to see birds.
Contact also: **Avesuruguay/Gupeca**

Canelones 1164, Montevideo, T02-902
8642, www.avesuruguay.org.uy.

Useful websites
www.welcomeuruguay.com Excellent
bilingual regional guide to all tourist related
businesses and events.
www.eltimon.com A good
Uruguayan portal.
www.turismodeluruguay.com A tourism
portal in English, Spanish and Portuguese.
www.brecha.com.uy *Brecha*, a progressive
weekly listing films, theatres and concerts
in Montevideo and provinces, US$2 (special
editions sometimes free). Recommended.

Visas and immigration
A passport is necessary for entry except for
nationals of most Latin American countries
and citizens of the USA, who can get in with
national identity documents for stays of up
to 90 days. Nationals of the following
countries need a visa for a tourist visit of
less than 3 months: Albania, Armenia, China,
Egypt, Estonia, Guyana, India, Morrocco and
Russia. Visas cost US$42, and you need a
passport photo and a ticket out of Uruguay.
Visa processing may take 2-4 weeks. For
those living in a country with no Uruguayan
embassy, a visa can be applied for online and
collected at any Uruguayan consulate before
entering the country. Visas are valid for
90 days and usually single entry. Tourist cards
(obligatory for all tourists, obtainable on entry)
are valid for 3 months, extendable for a similar
period at the **Migraciones office** C Misiones
1513, T916 0471, www.dnm.minterior.gub.uy.

Weights and measures
Metric.

Working hours
Shops: Mon-Fri 1000-1900; Sat 1000-1300;
shopping malls: daily 1000-2200. In small
towns or non-tourist areas, there is a break
for lunch and siesta, between 1300 and 1600.

Businesses: 0830-1200, 1430-1830 or 1900. **Banks**: 1200-1700 in Montevideo (some till 1800); Mon-Fri 1300-1700 in Colonia; also in the afternoon in Punta del Este and elsewhere; banks close Sat. **Government offices**: Mon-Fri 1200-1800 in summer; Mon-Fri 1000-1700 (rest of the year).

Contents

Footprint features

At a glance

⟳ Time required 1-2 weeks.

✿ Best time Dec-Mar best. Carnival and Holy Week are the biggest festivals, particularly in Montevideo.

✖ When not to go Coastal resorts packed out in Jan and can be all shut up in Jun-Sep.

Uruguay

Montevideo

Montevideo is a modern city that feels like a town. Barrios retain their personality while the city gels into one. The main areas, from west to east are: the shipping port, downtown, several riverside and central neighbourhoods (Palermo, Punta Carretas, Pocitos), the suburbs and Carrasco International airport, all connected by the Rambla. Everything blends together – architecture, markets, restaurants, stores, malls, stadiums, parks and beaches – and you can find what you need in a short walk.

Montevideo, the capital, was officially founded in 1726 on a promontory between the Río de la Plata and an inner bay, though the fortifications have been destroyed. Spanish and Italian architecture, French and Art Deco styles can be seen, especially in Ciudad Vieja. The city not only dominates the country's commerce and culture: it accounts for 70% of industrial production and handles almost 90% of imports and exports. In January and February many locals leave for the string of seaside resorts to the east. The first football World Cup was held in Centenario Stadium and won by Uruguay in 1930.

Ins and outs → *Phone code: 02. Population: 1,325,968.*

Getting there   Carrasco International **airport** is east of the centre, with easy connections by bus or taxi (20-30 minutes to downtown). Many visitors arrive at the port by boat from Buenos Aires, or by boat to Colonia and then bus to the Tres Cruces bus terminal just north of downtown. Both port and terminal have good facilities and tourist information. ▸▸ *See also Transport, page 27.*

Getting around   The Ciudad Vieja can be explored on foot. From Plaza de la Independencia buses are plentiful along Avenida 18 de Julio, connecting all parts of the city. Taxis are also plentiful, affordable and generally trustworthy, although compact. *Remises* (private driver and car) can be rented by the hour. Full details are given in Local Transport, see below. **Note**   Street names are located on buildings, not street signs. Some plazas and streets are known by two names: for instance, Plaza de la Constitución is also called Plaza Matriz. It's a good idea to point out to a driver the location you want on a map and follow your routeas you go. Also, seemingly direct routes rarely exist owing to the many one-way streets and, outside the centre, non-grid layout.

Tourist offices   Tourist information for the whole country is at the **Tres Cruces bus terminal** ① *T409 7399, Mon-Fri 0800-2200, Sat-Sun 0900-2200* ; at the **Ministry of Tourism**

① *Rambla 25 de Agosto y Yacaré (next to the port), T1885 ext 100*, or nearby at Rambla 25 de Agosto 206 1000-1700; and at **Carrasco international airport** ① *T604 0386, 0800-2000*; which has good maps. For information on Montevideo, inside **Palacio Municipal** ① *18 de Julio y Ejido, T1950, 3171 or 1831, Mon-Fri 1000-1600*, all helpful. Check at the municipal website for weekend tours, www.monte video.gub.uy. For the **Tourist Police** ① *Colonia y Av del Libertador, T0800-8226. Guía del Ocio* is recommended; it's sold at news-stands on Fridays (US$0.90s) and has information on museums, cultural events and entertainment. See also www.pimba.com.uy, www.montevideo.com.uy, www.cartelera.com.uy, www.arom perlanoche.com, www.banda joven.com and www.eltimon.com.

Maps Best street maps of Montevideo are at the beginning of the *Guía Telefónica* (both white and yellow page volumes). Free maps in all tourist offices and some museums. *Eureka Guía De Montevideo* is recommended for streets, with index and bus routes (US$6 from bookshops and newspaper kiosks).

Sights → *For listings, see pages 20-30.*

City centre
In the **Ciudad Vieja** is the oldest square in Montevideo: the **Plaza de la Constitución** or **Matriz**. On one side is the **Catedral** (1790-1804), with the historic **Cabildo** (1804) ① *JC Gómez 1362, T915 9685, Tue-Fri 1230-1730, Sat 1100-1700, free*, opposite. It contains the **Museo y Archivo Histórico Nacional**. The Cabildo has several exhibition halls. On the south side is the **Club Uruguay** (built in 1888), which is worth a look inside. See also the unusual fountain (1881), surrounded by art and antique vendors under the sycamore trees.

West along Calle Rincón is the small **Plaza Zabala**, with a monument to Bruno Mauricio de Zabala, founder of the city. North of this Plaza are: the **Banco de la República** ① *Cerrito y Zabala* and the **Aduana** ① *Rambla 25 de Agosto*. Several historic houses belong to the Museo Histórico Nacional: **Casa de Montero-Roosen, Museo Romántico** ① *25 de Mayo 428, T915 5361, Tue-Fri 1100-1700, free,* first built in 1728, rebuilt by Antonio Montero in 1831, contains late 19th, early 20th century furniture, furnishings and portraits. **Museo Casa de Rivera** ① *Rincón 437, T915 1051, Mon-Fri 1100-1700, Sat 1000-1500, free*, is an 1850 mansion of the first president of the republic. Its rooms are dedicated to various stages of Uruguayan history. Also in the Ciudad Vieja is the **Palacio Taranco, Museo de Artes Decorativos** ① *25 de Mayo y 1 de Mayo, T915 6060, Tue-Sat 1230-1800, Sun 1400-1800, free,* whose garden overlooks Plaza Zabala, a palatial mansion in turn-of-the-20th-century French style, with sumptuously decorated rooms, and a museum of Islamic and Classical pottery and glass. It was first built as a theatre in 1793; in 1908 it was bought by the Ortiz de Taranco family.

The main port is near the Ciudad Vieja, with the docks three blocks north of Plaza Zabala. Three blocks south of the Plaza is the Río de la Plata. Cross the Rambla from the docks to visit the **Mercado del Puerto** (see Eating, page 22) and the adjacent **Museo Carnaval** ① *Rambla 25 de Agosto 1825, T916 5493, www.museodelcarnaval.org, Tue-Sun 1100-1700, US$3,* a small exhibition with colourful pictures and costumes from the February celebrations. Proceed south one block to Cerrito, east two blocks to the **Banco de la República** and church of **San Francisco** (1864) ① *Solís 1469,* south across Plaza Zabala to Peatonal Sarandí (pedestrian street) and east to Plaza de la Independencia (see next paragraph), stopping at the aforementioned historical sites as desired. Restoration efforts are slow but steady. Although safe by day, with many tourist police, common sense, even avoidance, at night is recommended.

Between the Ciudad Vieja and the new city is the largest of Montevideo's squares, **Plaza de la Independencia**, a short distance east of Plaza de la Constitución. Numerous cafés, shops and boutiques line Peatonal Sarandí. Two small pedestrian zones full of cafés, live music (mostly after 2300) and restaurants, Peatonal Bacacay and Policía Vieja, lead off Sarandí. Below his statue (1923) in the middle of Plaza de la Independencia is the subterranean marble mausoleum of Artigas. Just west of the plaza is **Museo Torres García** ① *Sarandí 683, T916 2663, Mon-Fri 0930-1930, Sat 1000-1800, bookshop, donation requested (US$2 or 5)*. It has an exhibition of the paintings of Joaquín Torres García (1874-1949), one of Uruguay's foremost contributors to the modern art movements of the 20th century, and five floors dedicated to temporary exhibitions of contemporary Uruguayan and international artists. At the eastern end is the **Palacio Salvo** ① *Plaza Independencia 846-848*, built 1923-28. The first skyscraper in Uruguay

Montevideo Ciudad Vieja & Centre

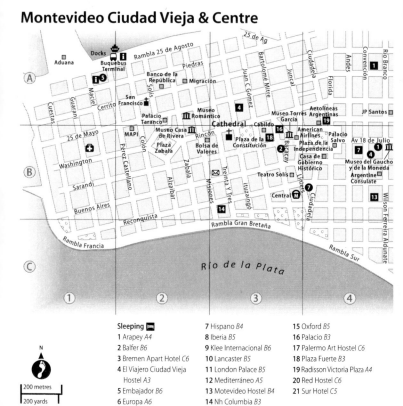

Sleeping

1 Arapey A4
2 Balfer B6
3 Bremen Apart Hotel C6
4 El Viajero Ciudad Vieja Hostel A3
5 Embajador B6
6 Europa A6
7 Hispano B4
8 Iberia B5
9 Klee Internacional B6
10 Lancaster B5
11 London Palace B5
12 Mediterráneo A5
13 Motevideo Hostel B4
14 Nh Columbia B3
15 Oxford B5
16 Palacio B3
17 Palermo Art Hostel C6
18 Plaza Fuerte B3
19 Radisson Victoria Plaza A4
20 Red Hostel C6
21 Sur Hotel C5

200 metres
200 yards

and the tallest South American structure of its time, opinions are divided on its architectural merit. Currently it houses a mixture of businesses and residences. The famous tango, *La Cumparsita*, was written in a former café at its base. On the southern side is the **Casa de Gobierno Histórico** ⓘ *Palacio Estévez, Mon-Fri 1100-1600*, with an exhibition of Uruguay's presidential history. Just off the plaza to the west is the splendid **Teatro Solís** (1842-69) ⓘ *Reconquista y Bartolomé Mitre, T1950 3323, www.teatrosolis. org.uy. Guided visits on Tue-Sun 1100, 1200, 1600 (Sat also at 1300), Wed free, otherwise US$2 for tours in English (US$1 in Spanish)*. It has been entirely restored to perfection, with added elevators, access for disabled people, marble flooring and impressive attention to detail. Built as an opera house, Teatro Solís is now used for many cultural events, including ballet, classical music, even tango performances. Check press for listings. Tickets sold daily 1500-2000.

Avenida 18 de Julio runs east from Plaza de la Independencia. The **Museo de Arte Contemporaneo** ⓘ *18 de Julio 965, T900 6662, Wed-Sun 1100-1600*, holds temporary exhibitions. The **Museo del Gaucho y de la Moneda** ⓘ *Av 18 de Julio 998, Edif Banco de la República, T900 8764, Mon-Fri 1000-1700, free*, was renovated in 2003. Museo de la Moneda has a survey of Uruguayan currency and a collection of Roman coins; Museo del Gaucho is a fascinating history of the Uruguayan gaucho and is highly recommended. Between Julio Herrera and Río Negro is the **Plaza Fabini**, or **del Entrevero**, with a statue of *gauchos* engaged in battle, the last big piece of work by sculptor José Belloni. Beneath the plaza is the **Centro Municipal de Exposiciones – Subte** ⓘ *Tue-Sun 1530-2100, free*, temporary exhibitions of contemporary art, photography, etc. In the **Plaza Cagancha** (or Plaza Libertad) is a statue of Peace. The restored **Mercado de la Abundancia** ⓘ *San José 1312*, is an attractive old market with handicrafts, meat restaurants and tango on Saturday and Sunday evenings. The **Palacio Municipal** (La Intendencia) is on the south side of Avenida 18 de Julio, just before it bends north, at the statue of **El Gaucho**. It often has interesting art and photo exhibitions and there is a huge satellite image of the city displayed on the main hall's floor. The road which forks south from the Gaucho is Constituyente, and leads to the beach at Pocitos. **Museo de Historia del Arte** ⓘ *Ejido 1326, T1950 2191, Tue-Sun 1200-1730* is also in the

Eating 🍴
1 Albahaca *B4*
2 Café Bacacay & Panini's *B3*
3 El Fogón *B5*
4 Los Leños Uruguayos *B5*
5 Mercado del Puerto *A1*
6 Subte Pizzerías *B6*
7 Tras Bambalinas *B4*

8 Viejo Sancho *B6*

Palacio Municipal. **Centro Municipal de Fotografía** ① *Palacio Municipal (San José 1360, T1950 1219), Mon-Fri 1000-1900, Sat 0930-1430,* has photography exhibitions.

The immense **Palacio Legislativo** ① *from Plaza Fabini head along Av del Libertador Brig Gen Juan Lavalleja (known as Av Libertador), 5 blocks east of Plaza de la Independencia (buses 150, 173, 175 from C Mercedes), free guided visits hourly Mon-Fri 0900-1800,* was built 1908-1925 from local marble: there are 52 colours of Uruguayan marble in the Salón de los Pasos Perdidos, 12 types of wood in the library. Other rooms are beautiful. Not far, and dramatically changing the city skyline, is the brand new 160-m high **Antel building** ① *Paraguay y Guatemala, Aguada, T928 0000, Mon, Wed, Fri 1530-1700; Tue, Thu 1030-1200, free,* with a public terrace on the 26th floor for panoramic bay views.

Outside the centre

Museo Nacional de Antropología ① *Av de las Instrucciones 948, Prado, T359 3353, Mon-Fri 1300-1800, Sat, Sun and holidays 1000-1800, free, take bus 149 from Ejido,* has a small, well-presented anthropological collection in the hall of a superb, late 19th-century mansion, the ex-Quinta de Mendilaharsu (see particularly the huge Chinese silk tapestry in the Music Room). On the same street, **Centro Cultural y Museo de la Memoria** ① *Av de las Instrucciones 1057, Prado, T355 5891, Tue-Sun 1200-1800, free,* is a fascinating space dedicated to remembering the horrors of Uruguay's 1970s-80s dictatorship. **Museo Municipal de Bellas Artes Juan Manuel Blanes** ① *Millán 4015, Prado, T336 2248, Tue-Sun 1215-1745, free, take buses 148 or 149 from Mercedes,* in the ex-Quinta Raffo (a late 19th-century mansion) is dedicated to the work of the artist Blanes (1830-1901). It also has a room of the works of Pedro Figari (1861-1938), a lawyer who painted strange, naive pictures of peasant life and negro ceremonies, also other Uruguayan artists' work. **Museo Zoológico** ① *Rambla República de Chile 4215, Buceo, T622 0258, Tue-Sun 1300-1715, free, take bus 104 from 18 de Julio,* is well displayed and arranged, recommended, great for children.

In the **Puerto del Buceo**, following the coast eastwards away from the centre, the ship's bell of *HMS Ajax* and rangefinder of the German pocket-battleship, *Graf Spee,* can be seen at the **Naval Museum** ① *Rambla Costanera y Luis A de Herrera, Buceo, T622 1084, 0800-1200, 1400-1800, closed Thu, free.* Both ships were involved in the Battle of the River Plate (13 December 1939) after which *Graf Spee* was scuttled off Montevideo. The museum also has displays of documentation from this battle, naval history from the War of Independence onwards and on the sailing ship *Capitán Miranda,* which circumnavigated the globe in 1937-1938. This ship is now in the port (can be visited weekends).

In **Parque Batlle y Ordóñez** (reached eastwards of Avenida 18 de Julio), are statues: the most interesting group is the well-known **La Carreta** monument, by José Belloni, showing three yoke of oxen drawing a wagon. In the grounds is the **Estadio Centenario**, the national 70,000-seater football stadium and a football museum, an athletics field and a bicycle race-track (bus 107). The **Planetarium** ① *next to the Jardín Zoológico, at Av Rivera 3275, www.montevideo.gub.uy/planetario, take bus 60 from Av 18 de Julio, or buses 141, 142 or 144 from San José,* gives good, 40-minute shows on Saturday and Sunday, free.

From the Palacio Legislativo, Avenida Agraciada runs northwest to **Parque Prado**, the oldest of the city's many parks, about 5 km from Avenida 18 de Julio (bus 125 and others). Among fine lawns, trees and lakes is a rose garden planted with 850 varieties, the monument of **La Diligencia** (the stage coach), the Círculo de Tenis and the Sociedad Rural premises. Part of the park is the adjacent **Jardín Botánico**. ① *daily summer 0700-1830,*

Wreckers, revolutionaries and gauchos

Uruguay's passion for rural life began in 1603 with Hernando Arias and the first shipment of cattle and horses to the Banda Oriental.

Today, a typical day on an *estancia* begins at the hearth, perhaps with a warming *mate*, before a horseride. The fireplace may be decorated with signs of present and past ownership, each brand burnt into the fireplace representing a personal history, but one element unites them all: the myth of the gaucho.

You might be forgiven for imagining yourself a latter-day gaucho as you put your foot in the *copa* (a cupped stirrup) and mount a sturdy Uruguayan horse, perhaps of the same breed as the one that Napoleon had shipped back to carry him around a wintry Europe. However, your thick poncho might well be the only piece of gaucho gear that you are wearing. Gauchos sometimes used ponchos as shields in knife fights, but on the ride you probably won't be needing a *facón* (a large dagger), nor a pair of *bombachas* (baggy trousers gathered at the ankle) or *culero* (an apron of soft leather tied around the waist, open on the left side) to avoid lacerations from a lasso during branding and gelding. Horses on tourism estancias are used to novice riders, and *rebenques* (short whips) are best kept unused by your side. You'll find the Uruguayan horse a compliant platform for launching your *boleadoras* (three stones, covered with hide, on ropes tied at the middle, are used for entangling the legs of cattle). At this point you may learn whether your horse is a *pingo*, a gaucho's favourite horse, or *flete*, an ordinary cargo beast. Riding along extensive *cuchillas* (ridges) and crossing rivers will bring to mind the nomadic gaucho lifestyle, and the revolutionary (largely gaucho) guerrilla bands. A *montonera* was a band of gauchos organized to drive the Brazilians and Argentinians out of Uruguay. Patriot leader Artigas was a gaucho-caudillo (boss).

Uruguayan life is built from livestock, sometimes quite literally. Houses were occasionally made from cattle hide. And cattle were put to other uses: coastal ranchers in Maldonado Department in the 19th century placed lights on the horns of their cows to lure ships onto the rocks for plunder.

---

winter 0700-1700, guided tours, T336 4005. It is reached via Av 19 de Abril (bus 522 from Ejido next to Palacio Municipal), or via Av Dr LA de Herrera (bus 147 from Paysandú). The largest and most popular park is **Parque Rodó**, on Rambla Presidente Wilson. Here are an open-air theatre, an amusement park, and a boating lake studded with islands. At the eastern end is the **Museo Nacional de Artes Visuales** ① *Tomás Giribaldi 2283, T711 6124, www.mnav.gub.uy, Tue-Sun 1400-1900, free*, a collection of contemporary plastic arts, plus a room devoted to Blanes. Recommended.

Within the city limits, the **Punta Carretas**, **Pocitos** and **Buceo** neighbourhoods are the nicest, with a mix of classical homes, tall condos, wonderful stores, services, restaurants, active beaches, parks, and two major malls. Outside the city along Rambla Sur, the affluent **Carrasco** suburb has large homes, quieter beaches, parks and services. **Parque Nacional Roosevelt**, a green belt stretching north, and the international airport are nearby. The express bus D1 (US$0.75) runs every 30 minutes along Avenida 18 de Julio and the Rambla and is about 30 minutes quicker to Carrasco.

At the western end of the bay is the **Cerro**, or hill ⓘ *getting there: bus from centre to Cerro: 125 'Cerro' from Mercedes*, 139 m high (from which Montevideo gets its name), with the Fortaleza General Artigas, an old fort, on the top. It is now the **Museo Militar** ⓘ *T487 3121, Mon-Fri 1000-1700, free (fort visit US$0.85)*. It houses historical mementos, documentation of the War of Independence and has one of the only panaramoic views of Montevideo. The Cerro is surmounted by the oldest lighthouse in the country (1804).

Bathing **beaches** stretch along Montevideo's water front, from Playa Ramírez in the west to Playa Carrasco in the east. The waterfront boulevard, Rambla Naciones Unidas, is named along its several stretches in honour of various nations. Bus 104 from Aduana, which goes along Avenida 18 de Julio, gives a pleasant ride (further inland in winter) past Pocitos, Punta Gorda and all the beaches to Playa Miramar, beyond Carrasco, total journey time from Pocitos to Carrasco, 35 minutes. The seawater, despite its muddy colour (sediment stirred up by the Río de la Plata), is safe to bathe in and the beaches are clean. Lifeguards are on duty during the summer months.

Montevideo listings

For Sleeping and Eating price codes and other relevant information, see pages 8-9.

⬤ Sleeping

Hotels may add 23% VAT, but it is usually included in the bill in cheaper and mid-range options; check when booking. High season is 15 Dec-15 Mar, book ahead; many beach hotels only offer full board during this time. After 1 Apr prices are reduced and some hotel dining rooms shut down. During Carnival, prices go up by 20%. The city is visited by Argentines at weekends: many hotels increase prices. Midweek prices may be lower than those posted. When not included, breakfast (*café completo*) costs US$2 or more. Most hotels above an **$** have cable TV and a mini bar or fridge.

The tourist office has information on the more expensive hotels. The **Holiday Inn**, hotel@holidayinn.com.uy, and **Ibis** groups are represented. For more information and reservations contact **Asociación de Hoteles y Restaurantes del Uruguay**, Gutiérrez Ruiz 1213, T908 0141, ahru@montevideo.com.uy.

City centre *p15, map p16*
$$$$ Radisson Victoria Plaza,
Plaza Independencia 759, T902 0111,
www.radisson.com/ montevideouy.
A/c, excellent restaurant (rooftop, fine views), less formal restaurant in lobby, luxurious casino in basement, with new 5-star wing, art gallery, business centre (for guests only).
$$$ Embajador, San José 1212, T902 0012,
www.hotelembajador.com. Sauna, swimming pool in the summer, TV with BBC World, excellent. Recommended.
$$$ Klee Internacional, San José 1303,
T902 0606. Very comfortable, good value in standard rooms, spacious, includes internet use, breakfast, a/c, heater, minibar, good view, satellite TV. Highly recommended.
$$$ London Palace, Río Negro 1278,
T902 0024, www.lphotel.com. Reliable, excellent breakfast, internet. Parking.
$$$ Nh Columbia, Rambla Gran Bretaña 473, T916 0001, www.nh-hotels.com.
1st class. Rooms have minibar and TV. Breakfast, restaurant, sauna, music show.
$$$ Oxford, Paraguay 1286, T902 0046,
www.hotel oxford.com.uy. Modern, good breakfast, safes, laundry service, parking. Recommended.

$$ Arapey, Av Uruguay 925, near Convención, T900 7032, www.arapey.com.uy. Slightly run down old building, but has character and good location, on route to airport. Variety of rooms with bath, TV, fan, heating, no breakfast.

$$ Balfer, Z Michelini 1328, T902 0135, www.hotelbalfer.com. Good, TV, safe deposit, excellent breakfast.

$$ Bremen Apart Hotel, Dr Aquiles Lanza 1168, T900 9641, www.bremenmontevideo. com. Recommended for short term rentals.

$$ El Viajero Ciudad Vieja Hostel, Ituzaingó 1436, T915 6192, www.ciudad viejahostel.com. Hostel with lots of services (Spanish lessons, bike hire,city tours, laundry, theatre tickets, football), shared bedrooms (**$**), free internet/Wi-Fi, safes, kitchen, airport transport, helpful staff. Recommended.

$$ Europa, Colonia 1341, T902 0045, www.hoteleuropa.com.uy. Comfortable, spacious rooms, good choice in this price range, restaurant, cybercafé, garage.

$$ Hispano, Convención 1317, T900 3816, www.hispanohotel.com. A/c, with breakfast, comfortable, laundry, parking.

$$ Iberia, Maldonado 1097, T901 3633, www.internet.com.uy/hoiberia. Very helpful staff, 1400 check-out, free bike rental, parking, Wi-Fi, stereos, minibar and cable in rooms. US$5.50 for breakfast. Modern, recently refurbished. Highly recommended.

$$ Lancaster, Plaza Cagancha 1334, T902 1054, www.lancasterhotel.com.uy. Central; needs a full renovation, but rooms are still quite acceptable with a/c, fridge, and some with nice views over Plaza Cagancha. With breakfast.

$$ Mediterráneo, Paraguay 1486, T900 5090, www.hotelmediterraneo.com.uy. With breakfast, TV, comfortable, boxy but clean rooms.

$$ Palacio, Bartolomé Mitre 1364, T916 3612, www.hotelpalacio.com.uy. Old hotel, a bit run down but safe, balconies, laundry service, stores luggage, no breakfast, frequently booked, good value. Recommended.

$$ Plaza Fuerte, Bartolomé Mitre 1361, T915 6651, www.plazafuerte.com. Restored 1913 building, historical monument, a/c, safe, internet, restaurant, pub.

$$ Red Hostel, San José 1406, T908 8514, www.redhostel.com. By the Intendencia, hostel with double rooms and dorms (**$**), all with shared bath, cheerful, cable TV, internet connection in rooms, computers, safe, breakfast, roof terrace and kitchen.

$$ Sur Hotel, Maldonado 1098, T908 2025, www.surhotel.com. Colourful, recently refurbished, welcoming, some rooms with balconies. Good continental breakfast, 24-hr room service, Wi-Fi.

$ Montevideo Hostel (members only), Canelones 935, T908 1324, www.monte videohostel.com.uy. Open all year, 24 hrs (seasonal variations, breakfast and internet included), dormitory style, kitchen, lots of hot water, but shortage of bathrooms and noisy, one bedroom (**$$**), bicycle hire US$2 per hr.

Outside the centre *p18*
Tres Cruces, Palermo

$$$ Days Inn, Acevedo Díaz 1821-23, T400 4840, www.daysinn.com.uy. A/c, breakfast, safe, coffee shop and health club, look for promotional offers.

$$ Tres Cruces, Miguelete 2356 esq Acevedo Díaz, T402 3474, www.hoteltres cruces.com.uy. A/c, TV, safe, café, decent buffet breakfast. Disabled access.

$ Palermo Art Hostel, Gaboto 1010, T410 6519, www.palermoarthostel.com. Cosy and colourful, with breakfast, bar and live music, private and shared rooms, some doubles (**$$**), near beach and US Embassy. Highly Recommended.

East of the centre
(Punta Carretas, Pocitos)

$$$$ Sheraton, Victor Solino 349, T710 2121, www.sheraton.com. Beside Shopping Punta Carretas, all facilities, good views, access to golf club. Recommended. Also a

Four Points Sheraton at Ejido 1275, T901 7000, in the centre (**$$$**).

$$$ Ermitage, Juan Benito Blanco 783, T710 4021, www.ermitagemontevideo.com. Near Pocitos beach, remodelled 1945 building, rooms, apartments and suites, some with great views, internet, buffet breakfast.

$$$ Pocitos Plaza, Juan Benito Blanco 640, Pocitos, T712 3939, www.pocitosplazahotel. com.uy. Modern building in pleasant residential district, next to the river, with large functional rooms, gym and sauna.

$ pp **Pocitos Hostel**, Av Sarmiento 2641 y Aguilar, T711 8780, www.pocitos-hostel.com. Rooms for 2 to 6 (mixed and women only), includes breakfast, use of kitchen, *parrilla*, towels extra, internet, Spanish classes.

Carrasco

$$$$ Belmont House, Av Rivera 6512, T600 0430, www.belmonthouse.com.uy. 5-star, includes breakfast, 28 beautifully furnished rooms, top quality, excellent restaurant Allegro, pub/bar Memories, pool, 3 blocks from beach. Recommended.

$$$$ Regency Suites, Gabriel Otero 6428, T600 1383, www.regency.com.uy. Good boutique-style hotel with all services, free internet, safety deposit, fitness centre, pool, restaurant *Tartufo* and pub/wine bar, a couple of blocks from the beach.

$$$ Cottage, Miraflores 1360, T600 1111, www.hotelcottage.com.uy. In a prime location next to wide beaches and in quiet residential surroundings, very comfortable, simply furnished rooms with fridge and a/c, restaurant, pool in a lovely garden. Excellent value.

② Eating

There is a 23% tax on restaurant bills that is usually included, plus a charge for bread and service (*cubierto*) that varies between US$1-3 pp.

City centre *p15, map p16*

$$$ El Mercado del Puerto, opposite the Aduana, Calle Piedras, between Maciel and Pérez Castellanos (take 'Aduana' bus), www.mercadodel puerto. com.uy. Don't miss eating at this 19th-century market building, open late on Sun, delicious grills cooked on huge charcoal grates (menus are limited to beef, chicken and fish, including swordfish). Best to go at lunchtime, especially Sat; the atmosphere's great. Inside the Mercado del Puerto, those recommended are: **Roldós**, sandwiches, most people start with a *medio medio* (half still, half sparkling white wine). **El Palenque**, famed as the finest restaurant. **La Estancia del Puerto**, **Cabaña Verónica**, **La Chacra del Puerto**. **Don Tiburón** has a bar inside and a more expensive and smart restaurant, **La Posada**, with tables outside.

$$$ Los Leños Uruguayos, San José 909, T900 2285. www.parrilla.com.uy. Good and smart *parrilla*, and also fish.

$$$ Panini's, Bacacay 1339 (also at 26 de Marzo 3586, Pocitos). Good Italian pasta. Large and lively.

$$ Café Bacacay, Bacacay 1310 y Buenos Aires. Good music and atmosphere, food served, try the specials. Recommended.

$$ El Fogón, San José 1080. Good value, very friendly, always full.

$$ Tras Bambalinas, Ciudadela 1250 y Soriano, T903 2090, www.trasbambalinas. com.uy. Colourful carnival-themed *parrilla*, also featuring pizzas, *picadas* and salads. Live music and stand-up often programmed. Very popular.

$$ Viejo Sancho, San José 1229. Excellent, popular, complimentary sherry or vermouth to early arrivals; set menus for US$6 pp.

$ Albahaca, W F Aldunate 1311, T900 6189, www.albahaca.com.uy. Open 0800-2000. Great lunchtime specials at this healthy, mostly-vegetarian café, very popular. Recommended.

$ Subte Pizzerías, Ejido 1327, T902 3050. An institution, cheap and good. Recommended.

$ Restaurant on 6th floor of YMCA building, Colonia 1870. Reasonable for lunch, with good views, ask for Asociación Cristiana de Jóvenes.

Centro Cultural Mercado de la Abundancia, San Jose 1312 (see Sights, above) has good authentic local eateries, with lunch specials. Highly recommended.

Outside the centre *p18*
In and around Pocitos

$$$ Da Pentella, Luis de la Torre 598, esq Francisco Ros, T712 0981. Amazing Italian and seafood, artistic ambience, great wines. Recommended.

$$$ Doña Flor, Artigas 1034. Classy French restaurant, limited menu but good, moves to Punta del Este in summer.

$$$ El Viejo y el Mar, Rambla Gandhi 400 block (on the coast), Punta Carretas, T710 5704. Fishing community atmosphere with a great location by the river.

$$$ La Spaghetteria 23, Scosería 2584, T711 4986. Very good Italian.

$$$ Tabare, Zorilla de San Martín 152/54, T712 3242. Wonderful restaurant in a converted old *almacén* (grocery shop). Great wines and entrées.

$$ La Otra, Tomás Diago y Juan Pérez, 2 blocks northeast of 21 de Septiembre in Punta Carretas. Specialises in meat, lively. Highly recommended.

$$ Pizza Trouville, 21 de Septiembre y Francisco Vidal. A traditional pizza place with tables outside, next to the beach.

$$ Tanquilo Bar, 21 de Septiembre 3104. Very popular restaurant/bar, great lunch menu.

Carrasco/Punta Gorda

Several restaurants on Av Arocena close to the beach, packed Sun middle day.

$$$ Café Misterio, Costa Rica 1700, esq Riviera, T6018765. Lots of choice on menu, sushi, cocktails. Completely new decor and menu every 6 months. Recommended.

$$$ Hacienda Las Palomas, P Murillo 6566. Tue-Sat evenings, Sun lunchtime. A little away from Carrasco beach, good Mexican restaurant and tequila bar.

$$$ Hemingway, Rambla Méjico on west side of Punta Gorda, T600 0121. Decent food, worth going for amazing sunset views of river and city, great outdoor seating.

$$$-$$ Bistró Latino, Dr Alejandro Schroeder 6415. Sushi, meats, pastas, seafoods, tapas, speciality cocktails. Highly recommended.

$$$-$$ García's, Arocena 1587, T600 2703. Spacious, indoor and outdoor seating, large wine selection, rack of lamb is a speciality. Recommended.

Confiterías Brasilero, Ituzaingó 1447, half a block from Plaza Matriz towards the port. Small entrance; easy to miss. A must, one of the oldest cafés in Montevideo and a permanent hangout of one of the greatest Latin American writers, Eduardo Galeano. Others include: **Amaretto**, 21 de Septiembre y Roque Graseras, Punta Carretas. Excellent Italian coffee and pastries. **Café Iberia**, Uruguay esq Florida. Locals' bar. **Conaprole Pocitos**, Rambla Gandhi y Solano Antuña. Ideal at sunset for riverviews, it serves very good strong coffee and quality Conaprole dairy products. A *completo* includes toasts, butter, jam, cheese, a slice of cake, biscuits, juice and coffee or tea, all for US$9.

Manchester Bar, 18 de Julio 899. Good for breakfasts. **Oro del Rhin**, Convención 1403. Mon-Fri 0830-2000 (Sat till 1400), open since 1927 it retains the feel of an elegant *confitería* serving good cakes and sandwiches or vegetable pies for lunch.

Café de la Pausa, Sarandí 493, upstairs. Closed Sun.

Options with multiple locations

Several good restaurants and establishments have locations in many neighbourhoods and serve typical Uruguayan fare. Among these are family restaurants: **La Pasiva**, **Pony Pisador**, **Don Pepperone** and **Il Mondo della Pizza**. A popular bakery chain is **Medialunas Calentitas**, great for coffee and croissants. Two popular *heladerías* are **La Cigale** and **Las Delicias**.

🎵 Bars and clubs

Montevideo *p14, map p16*
Boliches
See www.aromperlanoche.com for latest events and recommendations. Head to Sarandí, Bacacay or Bartolomé Mitre in Ciudad Vieja, or to Pocitos and Punta Carretas. Discos charge around US$5. Bars/discos/pubs offering typical local nightlife:
503 Bar, Aguilar 832, just north of Ellauri. Open all day 1930-0400. Pool tables, only steel tip dart bar in town, small wood frame entrance, no sign. **Almodobar**, Rincón 626, Ciudad Vieja. Fri, Sat 2230. Electronic and rock music.
Bancaria Jazz Club, Sarandí y Zabala p 5. Jazz sessions in the evenings.
Clyde's, Costa Rica y Rivera, Carrasco. Live music from 2000.
Fun-Fun, Ciudadela 1229, Ciudad Vieja, T915 8005. Hangout of local artists, founded in 1895, used to be frequented by Carlos Gardel, where *uvita*, the drink, was born. Great music Fri and Sat. Recommended.
Groove, Rambla República de Mexico 5521, Punta Gorda. Thu-Sat from 2400. Electronic music.
El Pony Pisador, Bartolomé Mitre 1326, Ciudad Vieja. Popular with the young crowd. Live music.
Viejo Mitre, Bartolomé Mitre 1321, Ciudad Vieja. Open till late all week. Mixed music, outside tables.

Outside the centre *p18*
Playa Ramírez (near Parque Rodó)
'W' Lounge, Rambla Wilson y Requena García. Fri-Sat 2300. Fashionable place for young people, live music on Sat, rock, electronica, Latin.

⚫ Entertainment

Montevideo *p14, map p16*
Cinema Blockbusters often appear soon after release in US, most others arrive weeks or months later. Most films are in English (except non-English and animated features). Modern malls (Montevideo Shopping, Punta Carretas, Portones) house several theatre companies each (Grupo Cines, MovieCenter, Hoyt's, and others). Independent art theatres: **Cine Universitario**, 2 halls: Lumière and Chaplin, Canelones 1280, also for classic and serious films. **Cinemateca** film club has 4 cinemas: 18, 18 de Julio 1286, T900 9056; Salas 1 y 2, Dr L. Carnelli 1311, T418 2460; Linterna Mágica, Soriano 1227, T902 8290; and Sala Pocitos, A Chucarro 1036, T703 7637. The Cinemateca shows great films from all over the world and has an extended archive. It organizes an international film festival, **Festival de invierno**. Entry is US$2.50 for 6 months, which may admit 2.

Tanguerías **El Milongón**, Gaboto 1810, T929 0594, www.elmilongon.com.uy. A show that may include dinner beforehand, Mon-Sat. For tango, milonga, candombe and local folk music. Recommended. **Joven Tango**, at Mercado de la Abundancia, Aquiles Lanza y San José, T901 5561. Cheap and atmospheric venue, Sun 2000. **Tabaris**, Tristán Narvaja 1518, T408 7856. Usually Fri, Sat 2200; check by phone. **Tango a Cielo Abierto**, Tango Under the Open Sky, in front of Café Facal, Paseo Yi and 18 de Julio, T908 7741 for information. Free and very good Uruguayan tango shows every day at noon on a wooden stage. Highly recommended. **La Escuela Universitaria de Música**, Sala

Zitarrosa, 18 de Julio 1012. Good, free classical music concerts.

Theatres Montevideo has a vibrant theatre scene. Most performances are only on Fri, Sat and Sun, others also on Thu. Apart from **Teatro Solís** (see Sights, above), recommended are **Teatro del Centro Carlos E Sheck**, Plaza Cagancha 1162/4, T902 8915, and **Teatro Victoria**, Río Negro y Uruguay, T901 9971. See listings in the daily press and *La Brecha*. Prices are around US$4; performances are almost exclusively in Spanish starting at 2100 or at 1900 on Sun. **Teatro Millington-Drake** at the Anglo (see Cultural centres) puts on occasional productions, as do the theatres of the Alianza Uruguay-Estados Unidos and the Alliance Française (addresses below). Many theatres close Jan-Feb.

○ Shopping

Montevideo *p14, map p16*
The main shopping area is Av 18 de Julio. Many international newspapers can be bought on the east side of Plaza Independencia.
Bookshops The Sun market on Tristán Narvaja and nearby streets is good for second-hand books. Every Dec daily in the evening is a Book and Engraving Fair, at Plazoleta Florencio Sánchez (Parque Rodó), with readings and concerts. The following have a few English and American books, but selection in Montevideo is poor: **Bookshop SRL**, JE Rodó 1671 (at Minas y Constituyente), T401 1010, www.bookshop. com.uy, Cristina Mosca. With English stock, very friendly staff, also at Ellauri 363 and at both Montevideo and Portones Shopping Centers; specializes in travel. **Ibana**, International Book and News Agency, Convención 1485. Specializes in foreign publications. **El Libro Inglés**, Cerrito 483, Ciudad Vieja. **Librería Papacito**, 18 de Julio 1409, T908 7250, www.libreriapapacito.com. Good selection of magazines and books, wide range of subjects from celebrity

autobiographies to art. **Puro Verso**, 18 de Julio 1199, T901 6429, puroverso@ adinet.com.uy. Very good selection is in Spanish, small secondhand section in English, excellent café, chess tables. It has another branch on Sarandí 675, **Más Puro Verso**. Others include: **Librería El Aleph**, Bartolomé Mitre 1358. Used and rare books in Spanish. **Linardi y Risso**, Juan Carlos Gómez 1435, Ciudad Vieja, lyrbooks@linardiyrisso.com. **Centro de la Cultura Uruguaya**, Plaza Fabini, T901 1714, www.corazon alsur.com.uy. Books on Uruguay in Spanish and Uruguayan music.
Galleries There are many good art galleries. **Galería Latina**, Sarandí 671, T916 3737, is one of the best, with its own art publishing house. Several art galleries and shops lie along C Pérez Castellanos, near Mercado del Puerto.
Handicrafts Suede and leather are good buys. There are several shops and workshops around Plaza Independencia. Amethysts, topazes, agate and quartz are mined and polished in Uruguay and are also good buys. For authentic, fairly-priced crafts there is a marquee on Plaza Cagancha (No 1365), and at Mercado de la Abundancia, San José 1312, T901 0550, auda@minetuy.com. For leather goods, walk around C San José y W Ferreira Aldunate. **Montevideo Leather Factory**, Plaza Independencia 832, www.monte videoleather factory.com. Recommended.
Manos del Uruguay, San José 1111, Sarandí y Bacacay, Ciudad Vieja, and at Shopping Centers, www.manos.com.uy. A non-profit organization that sells very good quality, handwoven woollen clothing and a great range of crafts, made by independent craftsmen and women from all over Uruguay.
Mundo Mineral, Sarandí 672. Recommended for amethysts, topazes, agate and quartz.
Markets Calle Tristán Narvaja (and nearby streets), opposite Facultad de Derecho on 18 de Julio. On Sun, 0800-1400, there is a large, crowded street market here, good for silver and copper, and all sorts of collectibles.
Plaza de la Constitución, a small Sat morning

market and a Sun antique fair are held here. **Villa Biarritz**, on Vásquez Ledesma near Parque Rodó, Punta Carretas. A big market selling fruit, vegetables, clothes and shoes (Tue and Sat 0900-1500, and Sun in Parque Rodó, 0800-1400).

Shopping malls The Montevideo **Shopping Center**, on the east edge of Pocitos (Herrera 1290 y Laguna, 1 block south of Rivera, www.montevideoshopping. com.uy). Open daily 1000-2000 and has a self-service restaurant, a cinema and *confiterías*. It also has wide range of shops selling leather goods, Foto Martín, bookshop, markets and more (bus 141 or 142 from San José). **Punta Carretas Shopping**, Ellauri 350, close to Playa Pocitos in the former prison, www.puntascarretasweb.com.uy. Open 1000-2200, is large, modern, with all types of shop, also cinema complex and good food patio, popular. Take bus 117 or 121 from Calle San José. Other shopping centres at Portones in Carrasco, www.portones.com.uy, the Tres Cruces bus station, www.trescruces.com.uy, and Plaza Arozena Shopping Mall.

▲ Activities and tours

Montevideo *p14, map p16*
Sports
Football (soccer) is the most popular. Seeing a game in **Centenario Stadium** is a must, located in Parque Batlle. If possible, attend a game with Uruguay's most popular teams, **Nacional** or **Peñarol**, or an international match. General admission tickets (US$5-10) can be bought outside before kickoff for sections Amsterdam, América, Colombes, Tribuna Olímpica. Crowds in Uruguay are much safer than other countries, but it's best to avoid the *plateas*, the end zones where the rowdiest fans chant and cheer. Sit in Tribuna Olímpica under or opposite the tower, at midfield. **Parque Central**, just north of Tres Cruces, **Nacional**'s home field, is the next best venue.

Other stadiums are quieter, safer and also fun. For information try www.tenfieldigital. com.uy, but asking a local is also advisable. **Basketball** is increasingly popular; games can be seen at any sports club (**Biguá** or **Trouville**, both in Punta Carretas/Pocitos neighbourhoods) or in **Estadio Cerrado Cilindrón** (the Cylinder), in the north city, in Villa Español. See www.fubb.org.uy for schedules. Rugby, volleyball, tennis, cycling, surfing (www.olasyvientos.com), windsurfing and kite surfing, lawn bowling, running, and walking are also popular. **Golf**: Uruguay has seven 18-hole and two 9-hole courses, between Fray Bentos and Punta del Este. Apart from Jan-Feb, Jul-Aug, you should have no problem getting onto the course, see www.aug.com.uy.

Tours
The **Asociación de Guías de Turismo de Montevideo**, agtmguias202@hotmail.com, runs historical and architecture tours of Ciudad Vieja leaving from the Cabildo every Sat. Check times and availability in English. Tours of the city are organized by the **Municipalidad**, see http://cultura. montevideo .gub.uy (go to Paseos) for details.

Day tours of Punta del Este are run by many travel agents and hotels, US$40-100 with meals.

Estancia tourism Information on *estancias* can be found at **Lares** (see below), which represents many *estancias* and *posadas*; at the tourist offices in Montevideo; or general travel agencies and those that specialize in this field: **Estancias Gauchas**, Cecilia Regules Viajes, agent for an organization of 80 estancias offering lunch and/or lodging, English, French and Portuguese spoken. Full list of estancias at www.turismo.gub.uy. Ask at these organizations about **horse riding**, too. **Cecilia Regules Viajes**, Bacacay 1334, T916 3011, T09-968 3608 (mob), www.ceciliaregules viajes.com, very good, knowledgeable, specialist in *estancia*, tango and railway tourism in Uruguay, and skiing in Argentina.

Jetmar, Plaza de la Independencia 725-7, T902 0793, info@jetmar.com.uy. A helpful tour operator.

JP Santos, Colonia 951, T902 0300, www.jpsantos.com.uy. Helpful agency.

Lares, Wilson Ferreira Aldunate 1341, T901 9120, www.lares.com.uy. Specializes in birdwatching and other nature tours, cultural tours, trekking, horse riding and estancia tourism.

Simply, Colonia 971, T900 8880, www.simply. com.uy. Adventure and nature tourism specialists, plus many other national and international packages.

Rumbos, Galería del Libertador, Rio Branco 1377, p 7, T900 2407, www.rumbos turismo.com. Caters specifically for independent travellers, very helpful.

TransHotel, Av 8 de Octubre 2252, T402 9935, www.e-transhotel.com. Accommodation, eco-tourism, sightseeing and tailor-made itineraries.

Turisport Ltda, San José 930, T902 0829, www.turisport.com.uy. American Express for travel and mail services, good; sells Amex dollar TCs on Amex card.

⊘ Transport

Montevideo *p14, map p16*
Air

The main airport is at Carrasco, 21 km outside the city, T601 1757, www.aic.com.uy; exchange facilities, but if closed, buses will accept US$ for fares to town. If making a hotel reservation, ask them to send a taxi to meet you; it's cheaper than taking an airport taxi. To Montevideo 30 mins by taxi or *remise* (US$12-21, depending on destination in the city – may be able to pay taxi driver in Argentine pesos or in US$, or charge it to hotel bill if without cash); about 50 mins by bus. Buses, Nos 700, 701, 704, 710 and 711, from Terminal Brum, Río Branco y Galicia, go

to the airport US$1 (crowded before and after school hours); dark brown 'Copsa' bus terminates at the airport. **COT** buses connect airport and Punta del Este, US$7.25. **Concorde Travel** (Robert Mountford), Germán Barbato 1358, apto 1302, T902 6346/8, has a service from hotel to plane (almost) US$10-25.

Air services to **Argentina**: for the Puente Aéreo to Buenos Aires, check in at Montevideo airport, pay departure tax and go to immigration to fill in an Argentine entry form before going through Uruguayan immigration. Get your stamp out of Uruguay, surrender the tourist card you received on entry and get your stamp into Argentina. There are no immigration checks on arrival at Aeroparque, Buenos Aires.

Bus
Local City buses are comfortable and convenient. Pay your fare to the driver or to conductor in the centre of the bus, US$0.85; buses D1 (see Sights Carrasco, above), D2, D3, 5, 8, 9, 10, 11 US$0.75. There are many buses to all parts from 18 de Julio; from other parts to the centre or old city, look for those marked 'Aduana'. For Punta Carretas from city centre take bus No 121 from Calle San José.

Remises: US$15 per hr; Remises Carrasco, T606 1412, www.remisescarrasco.com.uy; **Remises Elite** , T099-183802; **Remises Urbana**, T400 8665.

Long distance During summer holidays buses are often full; it is advisable to book in advance (also for Fri and weekend travel all year round).

Buses within Uruguay: excellent terminal, Tres Cruces, Bulevar Artigas y Av Italia, T408 8710 (10-15 mins by bus from the centre, Nos 21, 64, 180, 187, 188 – in Ciudad Vieja from in front of Teatro Solís); it has a shopping mall, tourist office, internet café, restaurants, left luggage (free for 2 hrs at a time, if you have a ticket for that day, then US$2 up to 4 hrs, 12-24 hrs US$4.75), post and phone offices, toilets, good medical centre, **Banco**

de Montevideo and **Indumex** cambio (accepts MasterCard). Visit www.trescruces.com.uy for bus schedules. Fares and journey times from the capital are given under destinations.

To Argentina (ferries and buses)
You need a passport when buying international tickets. Direct to **Buenos Aires**: **Buquebus**, at the docks, in old customs hall, Terminal Fluvio-Marítima; Terminal Tres Cruces, Local 28/29, and Punta Carretas Shopping, loc 219; in all cases T130. 1-3 daily, 3 hrs, US$69 tourist class, US$97 1st class, US$111 special; departure tax included in the price of tickets. At Montevideo dock, go to Preembarque 30 mins before departure, present ticket, then go to Migración for Uruguayan exit and Argentine entry formalities. The terminal is like an airport and the seats on the ferries are airplane seats. On board there is duty-free shopping, video and poor value food and drinks. **Services via Colonia**: bus/ ferry and catamaran services by **Buquebus**: from 5 crossings daily from 1 to 3 hrs from Colonia, depending on vessel, fares: US$21 tourist, US$60 1st class or US$47 on slowest *Eladia Isabel*, more expensive on fast vessels. All have 2½-hr bus connection Montevideo-Colonia from Tres Cruces. There are also bus connections to **Punta del Este**, 2 hrs, and La Paloma, 5 hrs, to/ from Montevideo. Cars are carried on either route, US$86-112 **Montevideo**, US$51-75 and 68-95 (depending on size of vehicle and boat) **Colonia**; motorcycles US$70 Montevideo, US$34-45 Colonia. Schedules and fares can be checked on www.buquebus. com. Fares increase in high season, Dec-Jan, when there are more sailings. Check the website for promotional discounts that may offer up to almost half the price. If you want to break your journey in Colonia, you will have to buy your own bus ticket in another company to complete the trip to/from Montevideo. **Colonia Express**, W Ferreira Aldunate 1341, T901 9597; also at Tres Cruces bus terminal, T408 8120, www.colonia

express.com, makes 2-3 crossings a day between Colonia and Buenos Aires in fast boats (no vehicles) with bus connections to/from Montevideo, Punta del Este and other Uruguayan towns. Fares, including Montevideo-Colonia bus: around US$47 via the website.

Services to **Carmelo** and **Tigre** (interesting trip): bus/ motor launch service by **Trans Uruguay/ Cacciola/Laderban**, 2 a day, at Tres Cruces T402 5721, www.cacciolaviajes.com/ www.transuruguay.com, US$32 (Montevideo to Buenos Aires via Carmelo and Tigre); US$18 boat from Carmelo to Tigre. Advanced booking is advisable on all services at busy periods. On through buses to Brazil and Argentina, you can expect full luggage checks both by day and night.

To Paraguay, Brazil, Chile   If intending to travel through Uruguay to Brazil, do not forget to have Uruguayan entry stamped in your passport when crossing from Argentina. Without it you will not be able to cross the Brazilian border. To **Asunción**, Paraguay, US$80, 14 hrs, Mon, Wed, Sat at 1300 with **EGA**, T402 5165 (and Río Branco 1417, T902 5335), recommended, meals served. Alternatively take bus to **Santa Fe**, Argentina (US$58, 10 hrs), via Paysandú bridge, for easy access to Asunción. The through bus route is via Paysandú, Salto, Bella Unión, Uruguaiana, Paso de los Libres, Posadas, Encarnación, to Asunción (there are no passport or customs formalities except passport checks at Bella Unión and at Encarnación). There are very comfortable buses to **Porto Alegre** (US$82, 12 hrs, Mon, Wed, Fri) and **São Paulo** (US$177, 30 hrs, daily except Sat. There is also a Sun service via Camboriú, US$134, 20 hrs, a good place to stop over, and Curitiba, US$153, 23 hrs) with **EGA** and **TTL** (**Tres Cruces** or **Río Branco** 1375, T401 1410/901 9050, www.ttl.com.br), neither daily. Buses to **Florianópolis** run Tue, Fri, Sat and Sun (US$125, 18 hrs). An alternative route (which avoids the risk of being stranded at the border by through-bus drivers) is to Chuy, **COT**, T409 4949, **Cynsa** T402 5363, or **Rutas del Sol**, T403 4657 (US$16, 5-6 hrs), then catch a bus to Porto Alegre (7½ hrs, US$33-40), either direct or via Pelotas. Some private tour companies in Montevideo offer excellent deals on overland bus tours to places like Iguazú, Rio de Janeiro, Salvador, Bariloche and Santiago (eg **MTUR Viajes**, www.mturviajes.com, recommended).

Taxi

The meter starts at about US$1 in *fichas*, which determine fares as shown on a table in taxi. Tipping is not expected but welcomed, usually by rounding up the fare. Do not expect change for large peso notes. Prices go up on Sat, Sun, holidays and late at night.

Train

Uruguayan railways, **AFE**, use outdated trains, but interesting rides for enthusiasts. The old train station has been abandoned, replaced by a nice new terminus next to the Antel skyscraper, known as **Nueva Estación Central** at Paraguay y Nicaragua (Aguada), T924 8080 or 924 9645, www.afe.com.uy. Passenger trains run Mon-Sat only along 2 lines, called 25 de Agosto and Sudriers. Most commuter trains run north between Montevideo and Progreso (about 7 a day), passing some of the country's poorest areas. Fewer services go beyond Progreso. Once a day, a service goes as far as San José de Mayo on the same line and once a day as far as Florida. Another commuter line runs northeast from Montevideo to Sudriers, passing Pando. To Progreso (50 min, US$0.80), to Canelones (1 hr 20 min, US$1), to Santa Lucía (1 hr 35 min, US$1.50), to 25 de Agosto (1 hr 40 min, US$1.50), to San José de Mayo (2½ hrs, US$2), to Pando (1 hr, US$0.80). Occasionally, long distance services and a steam-engine run for special events, such as the 48-hr celebration of the Día del Patrimonio (Heritage Day) in Oct. More information, T924 3924.

Montevideo *p14, map p16*
Airline offices Aerolíneas Argentinas, Plaza Independencia 749 bis, T902 3691 .**Air France/KLM**, Río Negro 1354, p 1, T902 5023, www.airfrance.com.uy. **American Airlines**, Sarandí 699 bis y Plaza Independencia, T916 3929. **ASATEJ Uruguay**, Student Flight Centre, Río Negro 1354, p 2, of 1 y 2, T908 0509. **Gol**, T606 0901, www.voegol.com. **Iberia**, Colonia 975, T908 1032. **LAN**, Colonia 993, p 4, T902 3881. **Pluna**, Colonia 1021, T902 1414, www.pluna.aero. **Tam Mercosur**, Plaza Cagancha 1335 of 804, T901 8451. For information on flight arrivals/departures, T604 0262, and www.tam.com.uy.
Banks Don't trust the few black market money changers offering temptingly good rates. Many are experienced confidence tricksters. **Casas de cambio** on Plaza Cagancha daily until 2200, including Sun; banks only open 1300-1700 (some till 1800). Find most banks along 25 de Mayo, Cerrito or Zabala, and on Plaza Matriz, in Ciudad Vieja, and in the centre along Av 18 de Julio. **Banred**, www.banred.com.uy, is the largest ATM network from where you can withdraw US$ or pesos with a Visa or MasterCard. **HSBC, Lloyds TSB, BBVA, Citibank** all have Banred ATMs. More ATMs in supermarkets. Airport bank daily 0700-2200. **Western Union**, throughout the city in **Abitab** agencies, some exchange houses, and **Disco** or **Devoto** supermarkets. Exchange houses along 18 de Julio, eg **Bacacay**, at 853, **La Favorita** (Amex agents) at 1497, **Suizo** at 1190, **Regul**, at 1126, or in Ciudad Vieja, eg **Continental**, Misiones 1472, **Globus**, 25 de Mayo 466, but shop around for best rates (rates for cash are better than for TCs, but both are often better than in banks, and quicker service). **Brimar**, Misiones 1476, and **Delta**, Río Negro 1341, have been recommended. **Car hire** It is wise to hire a

small car (1.3 litre engine) as Uruguay is relatively flat and gas prices are high. A small car can be negotiated for about US$60 per day, free mileage, including insurance and collision damage waiver, if you are hiring a car for at least 3 days (rates are lower out of season). Cheaper weekly rates available. Best to make reservations before arrival. **Autocar**, Mercedes 863, T900 5925, autocaruruguay@hotmail.com. Economical, helpful. **Punta Car**, Cerro Largo 1383, T900 2772, puntacar@puntacar.com.uy, also at Aeropuerto Carrasco. **Snappy**, Andes 1363, T900 7728, www.snappy .com.uy. **Sudancar**, Acevedo Díaz 1813, T402 6620, www.sudancar. com.uy. Most car companies don't allow their cars to be taken abroad. To travel to Argentina or Brazil, you can use **Maxicar** rentals in Salto, see page 44. **Cultural centres** Alianza Cultural Uruguay-Estados Unidos, Paraguay 1217, T902 5160, www.alianza.edu.uy, library Mon-Fri, 1400-2000, US publications (excellent selection), theatre, art gallery. **Instituto Cultural Anglo-Uruguayo** (known as the 'Anglo'), San José 1426, T902 3773, www.anglo.edu.uy (theatre, recommended, library Mon-Fri 0930-1200, 1430-1930); café at No 1227. **Alliance Française**, Blvr Artigas 1229, T400 0505, www.alianza francesa.edu.uy (theatre, concerts, library, excellent bookshop). **Goethe Institut**, Canelones 1524, T410 5813, www.goethe.de/montevideo (Mon, Tue, Thu, Fri 1000-1300, 1600-1930). **Instituto Italiano de Cultura**, Paraguay 1177, T900 3354, www.iicmonte video.esteri.it. **Centro Cultural de España**, Rincón 629, Ciudad Vieja, T915 2250, www.cce.org.uy, Mon-Fri 1130-2000, Sat 1130-1800, has art exhibitions and a café. **Internet** Cyber Café Nacho, Av del Libertador 1607 y Cerro Largo, T903 9070. Open till 2200, US$0.75 per hr. **Cyber Café The Night**, Vásquez 1418, T402 1715, US$0.65 per hr. Open till 0300. **Cyber Café Uruguay**, Colonia 1955. **Cyberi@**, San José 933. **Millennium Café**, Paraguay 1325, local 53, in mall. **Phone Box**, Andes 1363, US$0.80 per hr. **Zona Tec**, T908 9042, US$0.75 per hr. **Language schools** Academia Uruguay, Juan Carlos Gómez 1408, T915 2496, www.academia uruguay.com. **Medical services** Hospital Británico, Av Italia 2420, T487 1020. Recommended. **Post offices** Misiones 1328 y Buenos Aires; 0800-1800 Mon-Fri, 0800-1300 Sat and holidays. **Poste restante** at main post office will keep mail for 1 month. Next to Pluna office on Av Libertador, next to Montevideo Shopping Center, 0800-1300, and under Intendencia at cornerof Av 18 de Julio and Ejido, Mon-Fri 1000-2000, Sat 1700-2200. **Telephones** Antel, Fernández Crespo 1534 (headquarters) and at San José 1101 (Plaza), 18 de Julio 891 (Plaza Independencia), Arocena 1598 (Carrasco), Ariel 4914 (Sayago), Cádiz Garzón 1929 (Colón), José Belloni s/n (Piedras Blancas).

Western Uruguay

West of Montevideo, Route 1, part of the Pan-American Highway, heads to the UNESCO World Heritage Site of Colonia del Sacramento and the tranquil town of Carmelo. Off the road are the old British mining town of Conchillas and the Jesuit mission at Calera de las Huérfanas. Other roads lead to the Río Uruguay, Route 2 from Rosario to Fray Bentos, and Route 3 via San José de Mayo and Trinidad to the historic towns of Paysandú and Salto. The latter passes farms, man-made lakes and the river itself. There are also many hot-spring resorts.

Colonias Valdense and Suiza

Route 1 to Colonia de Sacramento is a four-lane highway. At Km 121 from Montevideo the road passes Colonia Valdense, a colony of Waldensians who still cling to some of the old customs of the Piedmontese Alps. For tourist information, T055-88412. A road branches off north here to Colonia Suiza, a Swiss settlement also known as **Nueva Helvecia** (*Population: 10,000, Phone code: 0552*), with lovely parks, gardens and countryside. In the town is the Santuario de Nuestra Señora De Schonstatt, all walls are covered by plants, and the first steam mill in Uruguay (1875).The Swiss national day is celebrated with great enthusiasm.

The highway skirts **Rosario** (*Phone code: 052*, 140 km from Montevideo, 60 km before Colonia del Sacramento), called 'the first Uruguayan Museum of Mural Art'. Dozens of impressive murals are dotted around the city, some with bullfights, some abstract designs.

Colonia del Sacramento → *Phone code: 052. Population: 22,000.*

ⓘ *All museums Fri-Mon 1115-1745, closed either Tue, Wed or Thu, except Archivo Regional (shut Sat-Sun), combined tickets US$2.50.*

Founded by Portuguese settlers from Brazil in 1680, Colonia del Sacramento was a centre for smuggling British goods across the Río de la Plata into the Spanish colonies during the 17th century. The small historic section juts into the Río de la Plata, while the modern town extends around a bay. It is a lively place with streets lined with plane trees, a pleasant Plaza 25 de Agosto and a grand Intendencia Municipal (Méndez y Avenida Gen Flores, the main street). The town is kept very trim. The best beach is Playa Ferrando, 1½ km to the east, easily accessible by foot or hired vehicle. There are regular connections by boat with Buenos Aires and a free port.

The **Barrio Histórico**, with its narrow streets (see Calle de los Suspiros), colonial buildings and reconstructed city walls, is charming because there are few such examples in this part of the continent. It has been declared Patrimonio Cultural de la Humanidad by UNESCO. The old town can be easily seen on foot in a day (wear comfortable shoes on the uneven cobbles), but spend one night there to experience the illuminations by nostalgic replica street lamps. The **Plaza Mayor** is especially picturesque and has parakeets in the palm trees. Grouped around it are the **Museo Municipal**, in a mid-18th-century Portuguese residence (with indigenous archaeology, historical items, natural history, palaeontology), the **Casa Nacarello** next door (18th century; depicting colonial life), the **Casa del Virrey** (in ruins), the **Museo Portugués** (1720) with, downstairs, an exhibition of beautiful old maps, and the ruins of the Convento de San Francisco, to which is attached the **Faro** (lighthouse, entry US$0.70, daily 1200-1800, on a clear day you can see Buenos Aires). The **Museo Naval** ① *Calle Henrique de la Peña y San Francisco, T25609*, was opened

Colonia del Sacramento

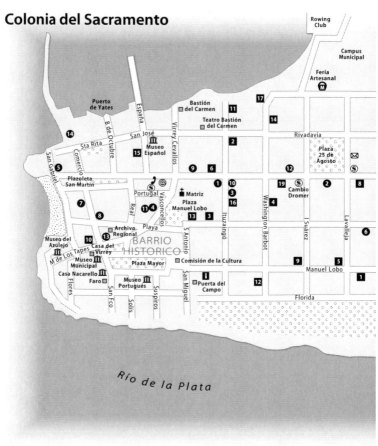

Sleeping 🛏

1 Blanca y Juan Carlos	8 Hostel Colonial	16 Posada Manuel de Lobo
2 Don Antonio Posada	9 Italiano	17 Radisson Colonia de
3 El Capullo Posada	10 Plaza Mayor	Sacramento & Restaurant
4 El Viajero	11 Posada de la Flor	Del Carmen
5 Español	12 Posada del Angel	18 Romi
6 Esperanza	13 Posada del Gobernador	19 Royal
7 Hostal de los Poetas	14 Posada del Río	
	15 Posada del Virrey	

at the end of 2009. At the Plaza's eastern end is the **Puerta del Campo**, the restored city gate and drawbridge. Just north of the Plaza Mayor is the **Archivo Regional** (1750), collection of maps, police records 1876-1898 and 19th-century watercolours. The **Iglesia Matriz**, on Calle Vasconcellos (beside the Plaza de Armas/Manuel Lobo), is the oldest church in Uruguay. Free concerts are held on Friday in the church grounds during the summer months. At the end of Calle Misiones de los Tapes, the Casa Portuguesa is now the tiny **Museo del Azulejo** (partly original floor, collection of French and Catalan tiles, plus the first Uruguayan tile from 1840). The house of Gen Mitre, Calles de San José y España, houses the **Museo Español** (closed for refurbishment, 2010).

At the north edge, the fortifications of the **Bastión del Carmen** can be seen; nearby is the Centro Cultural Bastión del Carmen, Rivadavia 223, in a 19th-century glue and soap factory, with frequent theatre productions. In the third week of January, festivities mark the founding of Colonia. The **Feria Artesanal** ① *Campus Municipal, Fosalba y Suárez*, is worth a visit. Kids will love the new **Acuario** in the Barrio Histórico ① *Calle Virrey Cevallos 236, esq Rivadavia, open Wed-Mon 1600-2000, US$1.50.*

Around the bay is **Real de San Carlos** ① *5 km, take 'Cotuc' or 'ABC' buses from Av Gral Flores, leaving Barrio Histórico, US$0.60*, an unusual, once grand but now sad tourist complex, built by Nicolás Mihanovic 1903-1912. The elegant bull-ring, in use for just two years, is falling apart (closed to visitors, bullfighting is banned in Uruguay). The casino, the nearest to Buenos Aires then (where gambling was prohibited), failed when a tax was imposed on Mihanovic's excursions; also disused is the huge Frontón court. Only the racecourse (Hipódromo) is still operational (free, except three annual races) and you can see the horses exercising on the beach.

Tourist offices ① *Flores y Rivera, T26141, daily 0900-1900 (closes at 2000 in peak summer and 1800 in winter), infoturismo@ colonia.gub.uy and www.coloniaturismo. com*, good maps of the Barrio Histórico and

Eating 🍴
1 Blanco y Negro
2 Club Colonia
3 El Asador
4 El Drugstore & Viejo Barrio
5 El Torreón
6 La Amistad
7 La Bodeguita
8 Lobo
9 Lo de Renata
10 Mercosur
11 Mesón de la Plaza
12 Parrillada El Portón
13 Pulpería Los Faroles
14 Yacht Club

the region. Beside the **Old Gate** ① *Manuel Lobo e Ituzaingó, T28506, daily 0800-2000 (0900-1900 in winter)*. Also an information desk at bus terminal. There is a **Ministry of Tourism** office at the passenger terminal at the dock, T24897, and a new tourist board set to open in 2010. Visit www.guiacolonia.com.uy, www.colonianet.com.

Conchillas, 50 km from Colonia and 40 km from Carmelo, is a former British mining town from the late 19th century. It preserves dozens of buildings constructed by C H Walker and Co Ltd. Tourist information is available at the **Casa de la Cultura** (daily 0800-1400) on Calle David Evans. The police station is also a good source of information. Direct buses from Colonia; road well marked on Route 21.

Carmelo → *Phone code: 0542. Population: 22,000.*

From Colonia, Route 21 heads northwest to Carmelo (77 km) on the banks of Arroyo Las Vacas. A fine avenue of trees leads to the river, crossed by the first swing bridge built 1912. Across the bridge is the Rambla de los Constituyentes and the Fuente de las Tentaciones. The church, museum and archive of El Carmen is on Plaza Artigas (named after the city's founder). In the Casa de la Cultura Ignacio Barrios (IMC), 19 de Abril 246, is a tourist office. Historically a mining centre, it is said that many luxurious buildings in Buenos Aires were made from the grey granite of Cerro Carmelo (mines flooded and used for watersports). It is one of the most important yachting centres on Río de la Plata and its microclimate produces much wine.

Calera de Las Huérfanas (Estancia de las Vacas) is the remains of one of the area's main Jesuit missions. Vines were introduced and lime was exported for the construction of Buenos Aires. After the expulsion of the Jesuits, it became an orphanage. It's in relatively good state and is best reached by car (exit from Route 21 clearly marked, some 10 km before Carmelo).

Between Carmelo and Nueva Palmira, another river port, is the colonial monument, **Capilla de Narbona** (Route 21, Km 263), built in the early 18th century. At **Granja y Bodega Narbona** (T540 4778), wine, cheese and other produce are available, as well as a fine restaurant and two exclusive hotel rooms. Nearby, at Km 262, is the luxurious **Four Seasons Resort**, www.fourseasons.com/carmelo.

Mercedes → *Phone code: 053. Population: 42,000.*

This livestock centre is best reached by Route 2 from the main Colonia-Montevideo highway. Founded in 1788, it is pleasant town on the Río Negro, a yachting and fishing centre during the season. Its charm (it is known as 'the city of flowers') derives from its Spanish-colonial appearance, though it is not as old as the older parts of Colonia. There is an attractive *costanera* (riverside drive).

West of town 4 km is the Parque Mauá, dating from 1757. It has a mansion which contains the **Museum of Palaeontology** ① *daily 1100-1800, free*, on the ground floor. The building is worth wandering around to see the exterior, upper apartments and stable block. Camping is possible in season. It takes 45 minutes to walk to the park, a pleasant route passing Calera Real on the riverbank, dating back to 1722, the oldest industrial ruins in the country (lime kilns hewn out of the sandstone). There is a **tourist office** at Colón, on the plaza, where maps and hotel lists are available.

Fray Bentos → *Phone code: 056. Population: 23,000.*

Route 2 continues westwards (34 km) to Fray Bentos, the main port on the east bank of Río Uruguay 193 km from Buenos Aires. Here in 1865 the Liebig company built its first factory producing meat extract. The original plant, much extended and known as **El Anglo**, has been restored as the **Museo de la Revolución Industrial** ⓘ *Tue-Sun 0800-1930, entry price includes 1½-hr guided tour 1000 and 1600, US$1.50, in Spanish, leaflet in English.* The office block in the factory has been preserved complete with its original fittings. Many machines can be seen. Within the complex is the Barrio Inglés, where workers were housed, and La Casa Grande, where the director lived. There are **beaches** to the northeast and southwest. **Tourist office**: 25 de Mayo 3400, T22233.

Crossing to Argentina

About 9 km upriver from Fray Bentos is the San Martín International Bridge. Owing to a long-running dispute between Argentina and Uruguay over a Uruguayan wood pulp mill, this crossing is effectively closed. Alternatives are at Paysandú, Salto, or one of the crossings on the Río de la Plata.

Paysandú → *Phone code: 072. Population: 74,575.*

North of Fray Bentos, 110 km, is this undulating, historic city on the east bank of the Río Uruguay. Along Route 3, it's 380 km from Montevideo. Summer temperatures can be up

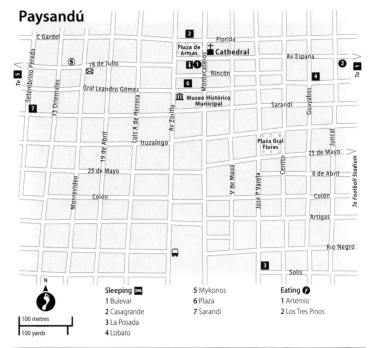

Paysandú

Sleeping 🛏	5 Mykonos	Eating 🍴
1 Bulevar	6 Plaza	1 Artemio
2 Casagrande	7 Sarandí	2 Los Tres Pinos
3 La Posada		
4 Lobato		

to 42°C. There is a 19th-century **basilica** ① *daily 0700-1145, 1600-2100*. The **Museo Histórico Municipal** ① *Zorrilla de San Martín y Leandro Gómez, Mon-Sat 0800-1300*, has good collection of guns and furniture from the time of the Brazilian siege of 1864-1865. **Museo de la Tradición** ① *north of town at the Balneario Municipal, 0900-1745 daily, reached by bus to Zona Industrial*, gaucho articles, is also worth a visit. **Tourist office** ① *Plaza de Constitución, 18 de Julio 1226, T26220, www.paysandu.com/turismo, Mon-Fri 0800-1900, Sat-Sun 0900-1900 (2000 in summer), and at Puente Gen Artigas, T27574.*

Around Paysandú

The **Termas del Guaviyú** *US$3.50, getting there: 50 mins by bus, US$3, 6 a day*, thermal springs 50 km north, with four pools, restaurant, 3 motels (**$$$-$$**) and private hotel (**$$**, **Villagio**) and excellent cheap camping facilities. Along Route 90, 84 km east, are the **Termas de Almirón** ① *T074-02203, www.guichon.com.uy*, five pools, with camping and motels. The **Meseta de Artigas** ① *90 km north of Paysandú, 13 km off the highway to Salto, no public transport, free*, is 45 m above the Río Uruguay, which here narrows and forms whirlpools at the rapids of El Hervidero. It was used as a base by General Artigas during the struggle for independence. The terrace has a fine view, but the rapids are not visible from the Meseta. The statue topped by Artigas' head is very original.

Crossing to Argentina

The José Artigas international bridge connects with Colón, Argentina (US$5 per car, return), 8 km away. Immigration for both countries is on the Uruguayan side in the same office. If travelling by bus, the driver gets off the bus with everyone's documents and a list of passengers to be checked by immigration officials.

Salto → *Phone code: 073. Population: 99,000.*

A centre for cultivating and processing oranges and other citrus fruit, Salto is a beautifully kept town 120 km by paved road north of Paysandú. The town's commercial area is on Calle Uruguay, between Plazas Artigas and Treinta y Tres. There are lovely historic streets and walks along the river. Next to Club Uruguay, Calle Uruguay, is the *Farmacia Fénix*, "la más antigua de Salto", over 100 years old. See the beautiful but run-down **Parque Solari** (Ruta Gral Artigas, northeast of the centre) and the **Parque Harriague** (south of the centre) with an open-air theatre. The **Museo de Bellas Artes y Artes Decorativas** ① *Uruguay 1067, T29898 ext 148, Tue-Sun 1500-2000 (Tue-Sun 1400-1900 in winter)*, in the French-style mansion of a rich *estanciero* (Palacio Gallino), is well worth a visit. **Museo del Hombre y La Tecnología** ① *Brasil 510, T29898, ext 151, Tue-Sun 1400-1900 (Tue-Sun 1300-1800 in winter), free entry and free guided tours in Spanish*, is very interesting, with a small archaeological museum. There is a Shrove Tuesday carnival. **Tourist office** ① *Uruguay 1052, T34096, www.salto .gub.uy, Mon-Sat 0800-1930*, free map; and at the international bridge, T28933.

The most popular tourist site in the area is the large **Presa de Salto Grande** dam and hydroelectric plant 20 km from Salto, built jointly by Argentina and Uruguay ① *taxi to dam US$20.50; tours can be arranged with SOMA, T20329*; small visitors centre at the plant. A road runs along the top of the dam to Argentina. By launch to the **Salto Chico** beach, fishing, camping.

Near the dam (2 km north on the Route 3) is **Parque Acuático Termas de Salto Grande** ① *open all year 1000-2000 (Jan and Feb 1000-2200), US$6, T30902, www.hotelhoracio*

quiroga. com/parque.htm, (4 ha) in a natural setting. There are several pools, slides, hydro massages, water jets and a man-made waterfall.

Crossing to Argentina
North of the town, at the Salto Grande dam, there is an international bridge to Concordia, Argentina, open 24 hours a day, all year. Passengers have to get off the bus to go through immigration procedures. Buses don't go on Sundays. Both Argentine and Uruguayan immigration offices are on the Argentine side.

Termas del Daymán and other springs
About 10 km south of Salto on Route 3, served by bus marked 'Termas' which leave from Calle Brasil every hours, are **Termas del Daymán**, a small town built around curative hot springs. It is a nice place to spend a night; few restaurants around the beautifully laid out pools. **Complejo Médico Hidrotermal Daymán** ① *T69090, www.mercotour.com/ complejodayman, therapeutical massage US$14 for 20 mins, US$23 for 40 mins, full day treatment from US$29*, has a spa and many specialized treatments in separate pools (external and internal), showers and jacuzzis.

The road to **Termas del Arapey** branches off the partially paved Route 3 to Bella Unión, at 61 km north of Salto, and then runs 35 km east and then south. Pampa birds, rheas and metre-long lizards in evidence. Termas del Arapey is on the Arapey river south of Isla Cabellos (Baltazar Brum). The waters at these famous thermal baths contain bicarbonated salts, calcium and magnesium.

To the Brazilian border: Artigas ➜ *Phone code: 0772.*
From near Bella Unión Route 30 runs east to Artigas, a frontier town in a cattle raising and agricultural area (excellent swimming upstream from the bridge). The town (*Population: 40,000*) is known for its good quality amethysts. There is a bridge across the Río Cuaraim to the Brazilian town of Quaraí. The Brazilian consul is at Lecueder 432, T5414, vcartigas@mre.gov.br. Border crossing is straightforward, but you cannot get a Brazilian entry stamp in Quaraí. You have to get it at the airport in Porto Alegre (daily bus Quaraí-Porto Alegre at 2100).

Western Uruguay listings

For Sleeping and Eating price codes and other relevant information, see pages 8-9.

⊝ Sleeping

Nueva Helvecia (Colonia Suiza) *p31*
$$$$ Nirvana, Av Batlle y Ordóñez, T44081, www.hotelnirvana.com. Restaurant (Swiss and traditional cuisine), half board available, see website for promotions, sports facilities, gardens. Recommended.
$$ Del Prado, Av G Imhoff, T44169, www.hoteldelprado.info. Open all year, huge buffet breakfast, TV, pool.

Camping Campsite in a park at the turnoff for Col Suiza, on main road, free, toilets, no showers.

Tourism farms
$$$ pp Finca Piedra, Ruta 23, Km 125, Mal Abrigo, northwest of San José de Mayo (convenient for Montevideo or Colonia), T0340-3118, www.fincapiedra.com. Price is full board, various rooms in different parts of this 1930s estancia and vineyard, lots of outdoor activities including riding, tours of the vines, winetasting, pool, caters for children, Wi-Fi.

$$$ La Vigna, T558 9234, Km 120 Ruta 51 to Playa Fomento, www.lavignalifestyle.com. Wonderful boutique eco-hotel, solar-powered and recycled furniture. Offers horse-riding and art lessons. Good food, all farm reared and organic. Owner is a cheese farmer, excellent produce. Highly recommended.

$$ El Terruño, Ruta 1, Km 140, 35 km before Colonia, T/F0550-6004. Price includes breakfast, horse-rides and activities.

$$ pp Estancia Don Miguel, Ruta 1 Km 121 y Ruta 52, T0550-2041, esmiguel@adinet. com.uy. Rustic, working farm, full board, transport extra, good activities, little English spoken.

Colonia del Sacramento *p31, map p32*
Choice is good including several recently renovated 19th-century posada hotels.

Barrio Histórico
$$$ El Capullo Posada, 18 de Julio 219, T30135, www.elcapullo.com. Spacious living area, English owners, stylish boutique-style rooms, outdoor pool and *parrilla*.

$$$ Plaza Mayor, Del Comercio 111, T23193, www.colonianet.com/plazamayor. In a 19th-century house, beautiful internal patio with lemon trees and Spanish fountain, lovely rooms with a/c or heating, English spoken.

Centre
$$$ Don Antonio Posada, Ituzaingó 232, T25344, www.posadadonantonio.com. 1870 building, buffet breakfast, a/c, TV, garden, pool, internet, Wi-Fi, excellent.

$$$ Esperanza, Gral Flores 237, T22922, www.hotelesperanzaspa.com. Charming, with sauna, heated pool and treatments.

$$$ Italiano, Intendente Suárez 105, T27878, www.hotelitaliano.com.uy. Open since 1928, it has been renovated with comfortable rooms, cheaper rates Mon-Thu. Large outdoor and indoor pools, gym, sauna, good restaurant. Recommended.

$$$ Posada de la Flor, Ituzaingó 268, T30794, www.posada-delaflor.com. At the quiet end of C Ituzaingó, next to the river and to the Barrio Histórico, simply decorated rooms on a charming patio and roof terrace with river views.

$$$ Posada del Angel, Washington Barbot 59, T24602, www.posadadelangel.net. Early 20th-century house, breakfast, pleasant, warm welcome, gym, sauna, pool.

$$$ Posada del Gobernador, 18 de Julio 205, T22918, www.delgobernador.com. Charming, with open air pool, garden and tea room open 1600-2000.

$$$ Posada del Virrey, España 217, T22223, www.posadadelvirrey.com. Large rooms, some with view over bay (cheaper with small bathroom and no balcony), with breakfast. Recommended.

$$$ Posada Manuel de Lobo, Ituzaingó 160, T22463, www.posadamanuelde lobo.com. Built in 1850. Large rooms, huge baths, parking, some smaller rooms, nice breakfast area inside and out.

$$$ Radisson Colonia de Sacramento, Washington Barbot 283, T30460, www.radisson colonia.com. Great location overlooking the jetty, casino attached. Internet, 2 pools, 1 indoor, very good.

$$$ Royal, General Flores 340, T22169, www.hotelroyalcolonia.com. Shabby lobby but pleasant rooms, some with Río de la Plata views, pool, noisy a/c but recommended.

$$ Blanca y Juan Carlos, Lobo 430, T24304. Member of an organization that arranges for visitors to stay with local families, welcoming, garden, safe, with breakfast. Recommended.

$$ Hostal de los Poetas, Mangarelli 677, T31643, hostaldelospoetas@hoteles colonia.com. Some distance from the Barrio Histórico but one of the cheapest, friendly owners, few simple bedrooms and a lovely breakfast room, tiny exuberant garden.

$$ Posada del Río, Washington Barbot 258, T23002, hdelrio@adinet.com.uy. A/c, small breakfast included, terrace overlooking bay.

$$ Romi, Rivera 236, T30456, www.hotel romi. com.uy. 19th-century posada-style downstairs, with lovely tiles at entrance. Airy modernist upstairs and simple rooms. Recommended.
$ pp El Viajero, Washington Barbot 164, T22683, http://elviajerocolonia.com. Small, friendly hostel with a/c and WiFi, **$** in dorm, HI affiliated, some doubles (**$$**).
$ Español, Manuel Lobo 377, T30759. Good value, shared bath in dorms, breakfast US$4, internet, kitchen. Recommended.
$ pp Hostel Colonial, Flores 440, T30347. Pretty patio and quirky touches, such as barber's chair in reception. Kitchen, bar with set meals, free internet access and use of bikes (all ancient), run down and noisy, but popular. Some doubles.
Camping $ Municipal site at Real de San Carlos, T24500, US$5 pp, in mini-cabañas, electric hook-ups, 100 m from beach, hot showers, open all year, safe, excellent. Recommended.

Carmelo *p34*
$$ Timabe, 19 de Abril y Solís, T5401, www.ciudad carmelo.com/timabe. Near the swing bridge, with a/c or fan, TV, dining room, parking, good.
Camping At Playa Seré, hot showers.

Mercedes *p34*
$$$ Rambla Hotel, Av Asencio 728, T30696, www.mercedesramblahotel.com.uy. Riverside 3-star hotel with quite good rooms and Wi-Fi.
$$ Ito, Eduardo V Haedo 184, T24919, www.sorianototal.com/hotelito/mercedes. htm. Basic though decent rooms with cable TV in an old house.
$ Hospedaje El Tigre, Sarandí 505, T28104. Simple, OK, clean showers.
$ Hospedaje Mercedes, F Sánchez 614, T23804, opposite hospital. Shared bath, very helpful.

Camping Club de Remeros, De la Ribera y Gomensoro (on the riverside), T22534. Also has dorm (**$** with own sheets), restaurant.
Tourism Farm $$$ pp Estancia La Sirena Marinas del Río Negro, Ruta 14, Km 4, T0530-2726, www.lasirena.com.uy. *Estancia* dating from 1830, picturesque, on the river, birdwatching, fishing, waterskiing, accommodation, meals, price is per person, full board (**$$ pp** with breakfast) friendly owners Rodney, Lucia and Patricia Bruce. Warmly recommended.

Fray Bentos *p35*
$$ Colonial, 25 de Mayo 3293, T22260, www.hotelcolonial.com.uy. Attractive old building with patio. Price includes breakfast.
$$ Las Cañas, 8 km south, T22224, lascanas@adinet.com.uy. A tourist complex with a beach; pleasant, but crowded in summer. Accommodation in motel rooms with kitchenette and bath, cheaper without kitchen, all with a/c, TV, fridge. Camping US$10 per day minimum.
$$ Plaza, 18 de Julio y 25 de Mayo, T22363, www.grupocarminatti.com/hot1ha.html. Comfortable, a/c, TV, internet, with breakfast, on the Plaza Constitución.
Camping At the **Club Remeros**, near the river and at Colegio Laureles, 1 km from centre, T22236.

Paysandú *p35, map p35*
Book hotels in advance during Holy Week.
$$$ Casa Grande, Florida 1221, Plaza Constitución, T24994, www.paysandu.com/ hotelcasagrande/. A/c, welcoming, parking, very good.
$$$ Mykonos, 18 de Julio 768, T20255. Buffet breakfast, meeting room, cable TV.
$$ Bulevar, Bulevar Artigas 960, T28835. Bar, garage, internet, cable TV.
$$ Lobato, Leandro Gómez 1415, T22241, hotellobato@adinet.com.uy. With breakfast, a/c, modern, good.

$$ La Posada, José Pedro Varela 566, T27879. Internet, patio with BBQ, a/c, restaurant and bar.
$$ Plaza, Leandro Gómez 1211, T22022, www.hotel plaza.com.uy. A/c, balcony, breakfast, parking.
$$ Sarandí, Sarandí 931, T23465. Good, comfortable, breakfast not included.
Camping Balneario Municipal, 2 km north of centre, by the river, no facilities. **Camping Club de Pescadores**, Rambla Costanera Norte, T22885, US$7 per day, showers. Also at Parque Municipal.
Tourism farms $$$ pp La Calera, near Guichón, 150 km east of Paysandú, T409 7856, www.lacalera.com. 40 luxurious suites with fireplace and kitchenette, pool, riding, rodeo, conference facilities. Self-catering. Highly recommended.
$$$ Estancia La Paz, 15 km south of Paysandú, T720 2272, www.estancialapaz. com.uy. Excellent rustic rooms, pool, customized gaucho experiences, horseriding, birdwatching. Highly recommended.

Salto *p36*
$$$ Hotel Horacio Quiroga, near Salto Chico, T34411, www.hotelhoracioquiroga.com. Best in town although some distance from centre, at the Termas complex, sports facilities, staffed by nearby catering school, special packages in season.
$$ Argentina, Uruguay 892, T29931. With breakfast, a/c, cafetería, comfortable.
$$ pp Concordia, Uruguay 749, T32735. Oldest hotel in Uruguay, founded 1860, Carlos Gardel stayed here, fine courtyard, pleasant breakfast room.
$$ Hostal del Jardín, Colón 47, T24274, hostalj@adinet.com.uy. Comfortable, TV, fridge, very helpful, spacious garden.
$$ Los Cedros, Uruguay 657, T33984. In centre, comfortable 3-star hotel, internet, buffet breakfast, conference room.

Termas del Daymán *p37*
$$$ Termas de San Nicanor, 12 km from Termas de Daymán, Km 485, Route 3, T0730-2209, www.termassannicanor.com. Estancia and gaucho experience, excellent nature watching, private pool. Recommended. Also camping (US$10 pp), good facilities.
$$ Del Pasaje, various addresses near Ruta 3, T69661, www.hoteldelpasaje.com. Hotel rooms, apartments for 2,4, 6 or 7 people and cabañas. Situated in front of the Parque Acuático Acuamanía.
$$ La Posta del Daymán, Ruta 3, Km 487, T69801, www.lapostadeldayman.com. A/c, half-board or breakfast only (**$** low season, hostel half price), thermal water in more expensive rooms, thermal pool, good restaurant, long-stay discounts, camping. Recommended. Also hydrothermal complex.
$ Bungalows El Puente, near the bridge over Río Dayman, T69271, includes discount to thermal baths.
$ Estancia La Casona del Daymán, 3 km east of the bridge at Daymán, T073-02137. Well-preserved, but non-operational farm, horse riding.
$ pp La Canela, Los Sauces entre Los Molles y Calle 1, T69121. Good value.
Camping See Termas de San Niconor, above.

Termas del Arapey
$$$ Hotel Termas de Arapey, T0768-2441, www.hoteltermasdelarapey.com. Open all year, a/c, TV, safe, indoor/outdoor pool, restaurant.
Camping US$5 pp, good facilities

Artigas *p37*
There are a few hotels in town and the **Club Deportivo Artigas**, Pte Berreta and LA de Herrera, 4 km from city, T0772-3860/2532, open all year, rooms (**$**) and camping (US$4.50 pp), restaurant, no cooking facilities.
Camping At Club Zorrilla, T4341.

Nueva Helvecia (Colonia Suiza) *p31*
$$-$ Don Juan, main plaza. Snack bar/
restaurant excellent food, pastries and bread.

Colonia del Sacramento *p31, map p32*
$$$ Blanco y Negro, Gen Flores 248,
T22236, www.bynrestojazz.com.uy. Closed
Tue-Wed. Set in historic brick building, smart,
great range of meat dishes, live jazz every
night. Cellar of local wines.
$$$ Del Carmen, Washington Barbot 283,
T30460. Open from breakfast to dinner,
fantastic views, great for evening drink.
Recommended.
$$$ Lo de Renata, Flores 227, T31061.
Open daily. Popular for its lunchtime buffet
of meats and salads.
$$$ Mesón de la Plaza, Vasconcellos 153,
T24807. 140-year old house with a leafy
courtyard, elegant dining, good traditional food.
$$$ Viejo Barrio (VB), Vasconcellos 169,
T25399. Closed Wed. Very good for home-
made pastas and fish, renowned live shows.
$$$ Yacht Club (Puerto de Yates), T31354.
Ideal at sunset with wonderful view of the
bay. Good fish.
$$ Club Colonia, Gen Flores 382, T22189.
Good value, frequented by locals.
$$ El Drugstore, Portugal 174, T25241.
Hip, fusion food: Latin American, European,
Japanese, good, creative varied menu, good
salads and fresh vegetables. Music and show.
$$ El Torreón, end of Av Gen Flores, T31524.
One of the best places to enjoy a sunset meal
with views of the river. Also a café serving
toasties and cakes.
$$ La Amistad, 18 de Julio 448.
Good local grill.
$$ La Bodeguita, Del Comercio 167, T25329.
Tue-Sun evenings and Sat-Sun lunch. Its
terrace on the river is the main attraction
of this lively pizza place that serves also
good *chivitos* and pasta.
$$ Lobo, Del Comercio y De la Playa, T29245.

Modern interior, good range of salads, pastas
and meat. Live music at weekends.
$$ Mercosur, Flores y Ituzaingó, T24200.
Popular, varied dishes. Also café serving
homemade cakes.
$$ Parrillada El Portón, Gral Flores 333,
T25318. Best parrillada in town. Small,
relatively smart, good atmosphere. House
speciality is offal.
$$ Pulpería de los Faroles, Misiones de
los Tapes 101, T30271. Very inviting tables
(candlelit at night) on the cobbled streets
for a varied menú that includes tasty salads,
seafood and local wines.
$$-$ El Asador, Ituzaingó 168. Good
parrillada and pasta, nice atmosphere, value
for money.
Arcoiris, Av Gral Flores at Plaza 25 de Agosto.
Very good ice cream.

Mercedes *p34*
The following serve good food: **La Brasa**,
Artigas 426. **Círculo Policial**, C 25 de Mayo.
El Emporio de los Panchos, Roosevelt 711.

Fray Bentos *p35*
$$ Los Paraísos, Inglaterra y Brasil,
T27996. Meat and pasta dishes.
Several other cafés and pizzerías on
18 de Julio near Plaza Constitución.

Paysandú *p35, map p35*
$$ Artemio, 18 de Julio 1248. Simple,
reputation for serving "best food in town"
$$ Los Tres Pinos, Av España 1474.
Parrillada, very good.

Salto *p36*
$$ La Caldera, Uruguay 221, T24648.
Closed Mon lunchtime. Good *parillada*,
also seafood.
$$ Pizzería La Farola, Brasil 895 esq Soca.
$$-$ La Casa de Llamas, Chiazzaro 20. Pasta.
$ Club de Uruguay, Uruguay 754. Breakfast
and good-value meals.
Trouville, Uruguay 702. Pizzería.

Colonia del Sacramento *p31, map p32*
There's a large artist community, Uruguayan and international, with good galleries across town. **El Almacén**, Real 150, creative gifts. Decorative pottery by local artist Eduardo Acosta at **Paseo del Sol**, Del Comercio 158. **Oveja Negra**, De la Playa 114, recommended for woollen and leather clothes. Leather shops on C Santa Rita, next to Yacht Club. **Afro**, 18 de Julio 246, *candombe* culture items from local black community, percussion lessons. **Colonia Shopping**, Av Roosevelt 458, shopping mall on main road out of town (east) selling international fashion brands.

Colonia del Sacramento *p31, map p32*
City tours available with **Destino Viajes**, General Flores 341, T25343, destinoviajes@adinet.com.uy, or or guided tours with **Sacramento Tour**, Av Flores y Rivera, T23148, sacratur@adinet.com.uy. **Asociación Guías de Colonia**, T22309/22796, asociacionguiascolonia @gmail.com, organizes walking tours (1 hr, US$5) in the Barrio Histórico, daily 1100 and 1500 from tourist office next to Old Gate.

Paysandú *p35, map p35*
Bodega Leonardo Falcone, Av Wilson Aldunate y Young, T072-27718, www.bodega leonardo falcone.com.uy. Winery tours at one of Uruguay's finest wine makers.

Nueva Helvecia (Colonia Suiza) *p31*
Bus Montevideo-Colonia Suiza, frequent, with **COT**, 2-2½ hrs, US$6.50; **Turil**, goes to Colonia Suiza and Valdense; to **Colonia del Sacramento**, frequent, 1 hr, US$3.50. Local services between Colonia Valdense and Nueva Helvecia connect with Montevideo/Colonia del Sacramento buses.

Colonia del Sacramento *p31, map p32*
Air Flights to Aeroparque, **Buenos Aires**, most days, generally quicker than hydrofoil. The airport is 17 km out of town along Route 1; for taxi to Colonia, buy ticket in building next to arrivals, US$10.

Road Roadworks on Route 1 west of Montevideo may delay traffic. There are plenty of filling stations. If driving north to Paysandú and Salto, especially on Route 3, fill up with fuel and drinking water at every opportunity, stations are few and far between. From Colonia to Punta del Este by passing Montevideo: take Ruta 11 at Ecilda Paullier, passing through San José de Mayo, Santa Lucía and Canelones, joining the Interbalnearia at Km 46.

Bus All leave from bus terminal between the ferry port and the petrol station (free luggage lockers, ATM, exchange, café and internet). To **Montevideo**, several services daily, 2¼-2¾ hrs, **COT**, T23121, **Chadre** and Turil, T25246, US$9. **Turil** to Col Valdense, US$3. **Chadre** to Conchillas, US$2.50. To **Carmelo**, 1½ hrs, **Chadre** and Berrutti, US$4. **Chadre** to Mercedes, US$9, Fray Bentos, US$11, Paysandú, US$17 and Salto, 8 hrs, US$23. **Turil** to Tacuarembó, US$29, Rivera, US$34, and Artigas, US$39. **Nossar**, T22934, to Durazno, US$10.

Ferry Book in advance for all sailings in summer. A new terminal opened in 2009. To **Buenos Aires**: from 5 crossings daily, with **Buquebus** (T22975), cars carried, fares and schedules given under Montevideo, Transport. **Colonia Express**, office at the port, T29677, www.colonia express.com, makes 2-3 crossings a day between Colonia and **Buenos Aires** (50 min) in fast boats (no vehicles carried) with bus connections to/from Montevideo, Punta del Este and Uruguayan towns: US$36 Buenos Aires to

Colonia (much cheaper if bought in advance online). **Líneas Delta** run a daily bus/boat service, 1245 (Sat-Sun 1400), to Tigre, US$28. **Note** Passports must be stamped and Argentine departure tax paid even if only visiting Colonia for 1 day.

Taxi A Méndez y Gral Flores, T22920; Av Flores y Suárez (on plaza), T22556.

Carmelo *p34*
Bus To **Montevideo**, US$12, Intertur, Chadre and Sabelín. To **Fray Bentos**, **Salto**, with **Chadre** from main plaza 0655, 1540. To **Colonia**, see above. To **Argentina**: via Tigre, across the Paraná delta, an interesting bus/boat ride past innumerable islands: **Cacciola** 2 a day; office in Carmelo, Wilson Ferreira 263, T542 7551, www.cacciolaviajes. com (the Uruguayan company on this route is **Laderban**), see Montevideo page 28.

Mercedes *p34*
Bus To **Paysandú**, with Sabelín, in bus terminal, T3937, 1½ hrs, US$6; also **Chadre** on the Montevideo-Bella Unión route. To **Montevideo**, US$15, 3½ hrs, CUT, Artigas (on plaza, also to **Argentina**), Agencia Central and Sabelín.

Fray Bentos *p35*
Bus Terminal at 18 de Julio y Blanes. To/from **Montevideo**, CUT, 4 hrs, 5 a day, US$16, also Agencia Central. To **Mercedes**, ETA, US$1.50, 5 daily.

Crossing to Argentina: Fray Bentos *p35*
Bus This border has been closed on and off since 2007. To **Buenos Aires**, 6 hrs, US$29.

Paysandú *p35, map p35*
Bus Can be hard to get a seat on buses going north. Terminal at Zorrilla y Artigas, T23225. To/from **Montevideo**, US$39

(**Núñez, Copay**, T22094, 4 a day), 5-6 hrs, also **Chadre**, **COT** and **Agencia Central**. To **Salto**, **Alonso**, T24318, US$6.50, 3 a day. To **Rivera**, US$11, **Copay**, 0400, 1700 Mon-Sat (Sun 1700 only). To **Fray Bentos**, 2 a day, 2 hrs direct, US$5. To **Colonia** by **Chadre**, 0750, 1750, 4 hrs, US$17.

Crossing to Argentina: Paysandú *p36*
Bus To **Colón** and **Concepción del Uruguay**, 3 a day (Copay 0815, 1645, Paccot 1545, 2030), on Sun Copay 1645, US$3.75 to Colón, US$4 to Concepción.

Salto *p36*
Bus Terminal 15 blocks east of centre at Batlle y Blandengues, café, shopping centre, *casa de cambio*. Take taxi to centre. To/from **Montevideo**, 6-7¾ hrs, US$25 (**Norteño**, **Núñez, Agencia Central** and **Chadre**). **Chadre** to **Termas del Arapey**, 1½ hrs, daily, US$3.50. **Paysandú** US$6.50, 1¾ hrs, 6 a day. To **Rivera**, US$20. To **Bella Unión**, 2 hrs, US$7.50, 2 a day. To **Colonia**, 0555, 1555, 8 hrs, US$23; to **Fray Bentos**, same times, US$11.50.

Crossing to Argentina: Salto *p36*
Bus To **Concordia**, Chadre (0800, 1400, return 1200, 1800) and **Flecha Bus**, 2 a day each, not Sun, US$7.50. To **Buenos Aires**, US$23, **Flecha Bus**.

Ferry To **Concordia**, Sanchristobal/Río Lago joint service, Mon-Fri 5 daily, Sat 3 daily, no service on Sun, US$4, depart port on C Brasil, 15 mins; immigration either side of river, quick and easy.

Artigas *p37*
Bus To **Salto**, 225 km, Oribe 279, US$10.50. **Turil** and others from **Montevideo** via Durazno, Paso de los Toros and Tacuarembó, US$31.50.

Colonia del Sacramento *p31, map p32*
Banks Banks open afternoon only. Most museums and restaurants accept Argentine pesos or US$, but rarely euros. **HSBC**, De Portugal 183 (Barrio Histórico), Mon-Fri 1300-1700. **Cambio Dromer**, Flores 350, T22070, Mon-Fri 0900-2000, Sat 0900-1800, Sun 1000-1300. **Cambio Colonia** and **Western Union**, Av Flores y Lavalleja, T25032.
Car hire In bus terminal: **Avis**, T29842, US$100 per day, **Hertz**, T29851, US$90 per day. **Thrifty** by port, also at Flores 172, T22939, where there are bicycles too (US$3per hr), scooters (US$7 per hr) and golf buggies (US$15 per hr) for hire, recommended as traffic is slow and easy to navigate. **Consulates** Argentine Consulate and Cultural Centre, Flores 209, T22093, open weekdays 1300-1800.
Internet Av Flores 172, US$1 per hr, or Av Flores 234, US$1.25 per hr. Bus terminal, US$2.70 per hr. **Post offices** On main plaza. **Telephones** Telecentro Sacramento, Av Flores 172.

Carmelo *p34*
Banks Banco de la República, Zorilla 361, for exchange and ATM.

Mercedes *p34*
Banks Cambio Fagalde, Giménez 709. Banco Comercial on Colón (just off plaza) and **Banco de la República**, on plaza.

Fray Bentos *p35*
Banks For exchange try Cambio Nelson, 18 de Julio y Roberto Young, T20409.

Paysandú *p35, map p35*
Banks *Casas de cambio* on 18 de Julio: **Cambio Fagalde**, No 1004; **Cambio Bacacay**, No 1008; change TCs, Sat 0830-1230. **Bancode la República**, 18 de Julio y Montevideo. **Consulates** Argentina, Gómez 1034, T22253, Mon-Fri 1300-1800. **Internet** paysandu.com, 18 de Julio 1250, plaza, US$2 per hr. **Post offices** Montevideo y 18 de Julio. **Telephones** Antel, Montevideo 875, T22100.

Salto *p36*
Banks Banco Comercial and Banco de la República, both on Uruguay. *casas de cambio* on Uruguay. **Car hire Maxicar**, Paraguay 764, T35554, 099-435454, maxirentsalto@hotmail.com. 24 hrs, cars allowed to travel to Argentina and Brazil. **Consulates** Argentina, Artigas 1162, T32931, Mon-Fri 0900-1400. **Post offices** Treinta y Tres y Artigas. **Scooter hire** Agraciada 2019, T29967.

Eastern Uruguay

Resorts line the coast from Montevideo to Punta del Este, the ultimate magnet for summer holidaymakers, especially from Argentina. Out of season, it is quieter and you can have the beaches to yourself, which is pretty much the case the closer you get to Brazil year round. Inland are cattle ranches, some of which welcome visitors, and hills with expansive views.

East from Montevideo → *For listings, see pages 50-57.*

This beautiful coast consists of an endless succession of small bays, beaches and promontories, set among hills and woods. The beach season is from December to the end of February. An excellent four-lane highway leads to Punta del Este and Rocha, and a good two-lane highway to Chuy. This route will give you a chance to see the most important Uruguayan beach resorts, as well as Parque Nacional Santa Teresa and other natural attractions. If driving there are three tolls each way (about US$2), but this route is the easiest and the most comfortable in Uruguay with sufficient service stations along the way.

Piriápolis → *Phone code: 043. Population: 6,000.*

This resort set among hills, 101 km from Montevideo, is laid out with an abundance of shady trees, and the district is rich in pine, eucalyptus and acacia woods. It has a good beach, a yacht harbour, a country club, a motor-racing track (street circuit) and is particularly popular with Argentines. It was, in fact, founded in the 1890s as a bathing resort for residents of Buenos Aires. Next to the marina is a small cable car (with seats for two) to the top of **Cerro San Antonio** ⓘ *US$4, 10 mins ride, free car park and toilets at lower station.* Magnificent views of Piriápolis and beaches, several restaurants. Recommended, but be careful when disembarking. North of the centre, at **Punta de Playa Colorada**, is a marine rescue centre ⓘ *sos-faunamarina@adinet.com.uy,* that looks after injured sea creatures before releasing them to the wild. **Tourist office**, Asociación de Turismo ⓘ *Paseo de la Pasiva, Rambla de los Argentinos, summer 0900-2400, winter 1000-1800, T25055/22560.*

About 6 km north on the R37 is **Cerro Pan de Azúcar** (Sugar Loaf Hill) ⓘ *getting there: take bus 'Cerro Pan de Azúcar' and get off after 6 km,* crowned by a tall cross with a circular stairway inside, fine coastal views. There is only a steep path, marked by red arrows, up to the cross. Just north of Piriápolis R 37 passes the La Cascada Municipal park (open all year) which contains the house of Francisco Piria, the founder of the resort, **Museo Castillo de Piria** ⓘ *open daily in summer, weekends in winter, 1000-2100.* About 4 km beyond Cerro Pan de Azúcar is the village of Pan de Azúcar, which has a **Museo al Aire Libre de Pintura** where the walls of the buildings have been decorated by Uruguayan and Argentine painters, designers and writers with humorous and tango themes (direct bus every hour from Piriápolis).

Portezuelo and Punta Ballena

R93 runs between the coast and the Laguna del Sauce to Portezuelo, which has good beaches. The **Arboreto Lussich** ① *T78077, 1030-1630*, on the west slope of the Sierra de la Ballena (north of R93) contains a unique set of native and exotic trees. There are footpaths, or you can drive through; two *miradores*; worth a visit. From Portezuelo drive north towards the R9 by way of the R12 which then continues, unpaved, to Minas. Just off R12 is **El Tambo Lapataia** ① *1 km east from Solanas, then 4 km north, T042-220000, www.lapataiapuntadeleste.com*, a dairy farm open to the public, selling ice cream, *dulce de leche*, homemade pizzas and pastas, with an international jazz festival in January.

At Punta Ballena there is a wide crescent beach, calm water and very clean sand. The place is a residential resort but is still quiet. At the top of Punta Ballena there is a panoramic road 2½ km long with remarkable views of the coast. **Casa Pueblo**, the house and gallery of Uruguayan artist Carlos Páez Vilaro, is built in a Spanish-Moroccan style on a cliff over the sea; the gallery can be visited (US$6), there are paintings, collages and ceramics on display, and for sale; open all year. Walk downhill towards the sea for a good view of the house.

Maldonado → *Phone code: 042. Population: 55,000.*

The capital of Maldonado Department, 140 km E of Montevideo, is a peaceful town, sacked by the British in 1806. It has many colonial remains and the historic centre was restored in 2005. It is also a dormitory suburb of Punta del Este. Worth seeing is the **El Vigia watch tower** ① *Gorriti y Pérez del Puerto*; the Cathedral (started 1801, completed 1895), on Plaza San Fernando; the windmill; the **Cuartel de Dragones exhibition centre** ① *Pérez del Puerto y 18 de Julio, by Plaza San Fernando*, and the **Cachimba del Rey** ① *on the continuation of 3 de Febrero, almost Artigas*, an old well – legend claims that those who drink from it will never leave Maldonado. **Museo Mazzoni** ① *Ituzaingó 687, T221107, Tue1600-2030, Wed-Sat 1030-2130, Sun 1300-2100*, has regional items, indigenous, Spanish, Portuguese and English. **Museo de Arte Americano** ① *José Dodera 648 y Treinta y Tres, T22276, 2000-2200, Dec and Feb Fri-Sun only (closed winter)*, a private museum of national and international art, interesting. **Tourist office** ① *Dirección General de Turismo, Edificio Municipal, T231773, www.maldonado.gub.uy*.

Punta del Este → *Phone code: 042.*

About 7 km from Maldonado and 139 km from Montevideo (a little less by dual carriageway), facing the bay on one side and the open waters of the Atlantic on the other, lies the largest and best known of the resorts, **Punta del Este**, which is particularly popular among Argentines and Brazilians. The narrow peninsula of Punta del Este has been entirely built over. On the land side, the city is flanked by large planted forests of eucalyptus, pine and mimosa. Two blocks from the sea, at the tip of the peninsula, is the historic monument of El Faro (lighthouse); in this part of the city no building may exceed its height. On the ocean side of the peninsula, at the end of Calle 25 (Arrecifes), is a shrine to the first mass said by the Conquistadores on this coast, 2 February 1515. Three blocks from the shrine is Plaza General Artigas, which has a *feria artesanal* (handicraft market); along its side runs Avenida Gorlero, the main street. There are two casinos, a golf course, and many beautiful holiday houses. **Museo Ralli of Contemporary Latin American Art** ① *Curupay y Los Arachanes, Barrio Beverly Hills, T483476, Tue-Sun 1700-2100 in Jan-Feb, Sat-Sun 1400-1800 rest of year, free*. Worth a visit but a car is needed.

Punta del Este has excellent bathing **beaches**, the calm *playa mansa* on the bay side, the rough *playa brava* on the ocean side. There are some small beaches hemmed in by rocks on this side of the peninsula, but most people go to where the extensive *playa brava* starts. Papa Charlie beach on the Atlantic (Parada 13) is preferred by families with small children as it is safe. Quieter beaches are at La Barra and beyond.

There is an excellent yacht marina, yacht and fishing clubs. There is good fishing both at sea and in three nearby lakes and the Río Maldonado. **Tourist information** ⓘ *Liga de Fomento, Parada 1, T446519, open summer 0900-2400, winter 1000-1800; in bus station T494042; at Parada 24, Playa Las Delicias (Mansa side), T230050; and at airports.* See the websites www.puntaweb.com, www.puntadeleste.com and www.vivapunta.com.

Isla de Gorriti, visited by explorers including Solís, Magellan and Drake, was heavily fortified by the Spanish in the 1760's to keep the Portuguese out. The island, densely wooded and with superb beaches, is an ideal spot for campers (boats from 0900-1700, return 1015-1815, US\$12.70, T446166; *Don Quico*, also does fishing trips, T448945). On **Isla de Lobos**, which is a government reserve within sight of the town, there is a huge sea-lion colony; excursions, US\$30-50. Ticket should be booked in advance (T441716). See also Activities and tours, below.

Beaches east of Punta del Este

Between the Peninsula and the mouth of the Río Maldonado, a road runs along the coast, passing luxurious houses, dunes and pines. Some of the most renowned architects of Uruguay and Argentina design houses here. The river is crossed by a unique undulating bridge, like a shallow M, to **La Barra**, a fashionable place, especially for summer nightlife, with beaches, art galleries, bars and restaurants (take a bus from Punta del Este terminal or taxi US\$20). The **Museo del Mar Sirenamis** ⓘ *1 km off the coast road, watch for signs, T771817, summer daily 1030-2000 winter 1100-1700,*

Punta del Este

Sleeping 🛏
1 1949 Hostel
2 Conrad
3 Gaudi
4 Iberia
5 Palace
6 Punta del Este Hostel
7 Remanso
8 Tánger

Eating 🍴
1 Cantón Chino

2 El Ciclista
3 Gure-etxe
4 Il Barreto
5 Isidora
6 Juana Enea
7 Lo de Charlie
8 Lo de Tere
9 Los Caracoles
10 Viejo Marino
11 Virazón
12 Yatch Club Uruguayo

US$5, has an excellent collection on the subject of the sea, its life and history and on the first beach resorts (it claims to have 5,000 exhibits). The coast road climbs a headland here before descending to the beaches further north, Montoya and **Manantiales** (reached by Condesa bus; taxi US$28). Some 30 km from Punta del Este is the fishing village of **Faro José Ignacio** with a lighthouse ① *summer daily 1100-2030, winter 1100-1330, 1430-1830, US$0.75*, a beach club and other new developments, now the road is paved. Coastal R10 runs some way east of José Ignacio, but there is no through connection to La Paloma as a new bridge across the mouth of the Lago Garzón is not operational. A car ferry sometimes runs; rowing boats will take pedestrians and cyclists across.

La Paloma and around → *Phone code: 0479. Population: 5,000.*

Protected by an island and a sandspit, this is a good port for yachts. The surrounding scenery is attractive, with extensive wetlands nearby. You can walk for miles along the beach. The pace is more relaxed than Punta del Este. **Tourist office** ① *Av Solari y C Paloma at entrance to town, T96088*, very helpful. For the Department of Rocha see www.turismorocha.gub.uy.

Coastal R10 runs to Aguas Dulces (regular bus services along this route). About 10 km from La Paloma is **La Pedrera**, a beautiful village with sandy beaches. Beyond La Pedrera the road runs near pleasant fishing villages which are rapidly being developed with holiday homes, for example **Barra de Valizas**, 50 minutes north. At **Cabo Polonio** (permanent population 80), visits to the islands of Castillos and Wolf can be arranged to see sea lions and penguins. It has two great beaches: the north beach is more rugged, while the south is tamer by comparison. Both have lifeguards on duty (though their zone of protection only covers a tiny portion of the kilometres and kilometres of beach). The village is part of a nature reserve. This limits the number of people who are allowed to stay there since the number of lodgings is limited and camping is strictly forbidden (if you arrive with a tent, it may be confiscated). During January or February (and especially during Carnival), you **have** to reserve a room in one of the few posadas or hotels, or better yet, rent a house (see Sleeping, below). From Km 264 on the main road all-terrain vehicles run 8 km across the dunes to the village (several companies, around US$5). Day visitors must leave just after sundown (see Transport, below). Ask locally in Valizas about walking there, 3-4 hours via the north beach (very interesting, but hot, unless you go early). There are also pine woods with paths leading to the beach or village.

The **Monte de Ombúes** ① *open in summer months, from Jan, free, basic restaurant with honest prices* is a wood containing a few *ombú* trees (Phytolacca dioica – the national tree), *coronilla* (Scutia buxifolia) and *canelón* (Rapanea laetevirens). It has a small circuit to follow and a good hide for birdwatching. To reach the woods from Km 264, go 2 km north along R10 to the bridge. Here take a boat with guide, 30 minutes along the river (*Monte Grande* recommended as they visit both sides of the river, montegrande@adinet.com.uy). You can also walk from Km 264 across the fields, but it's along way and the last 150 m are through thick brush. The bridge is 16 km from Castillos on R9 (see next paragraph): turn onto R16 towards Aguas Dulces, just before which you turn southwest onto R10.

From **Aguas Dulces** the road runs inland to the town of **Castillos** (easy bus connections to Chuy), where it rejoins R9. A tourist office at Aguas Dulces/Castillos crossroads on R9 has details on hotels.

Punta del Diablo

At Km 298 there is a turn to a fishing village in dramatic surroundings, again with fine beaches. Punta del Diablo is very rustic, popular with young people in high season, but from April to November the solitude and the dramatically lower prices make it a wonderful getaway for couples or families. Increased popularity has brought more lodging and services year round, although off-season activity is still extremely low compared to summer. **Note** there is no ATM in Punta del Diablo so bring enough cash with you. The nearest ATM is in Chuy. See www.portaldeldiablo.com.

Parque Nacional Santa Teresa

① *100 km from Rocha, 308 km from Montevideo, open 0700-1900 to day visitors (open 24 hrs for campers).*

This park has curving, palm-lined avenues and plantations of many exotic trees. It also contains botanical gardens, fresh-water pools for bathing and beaches which stretch for many kilometres (the surf is too rough for swimming). It is the site of the impressive colonial fortress of Santa Teresa, begun by the Portuguese in 1762 and seized by the Spanish in 1793. The fortress houses a **museum** of artefacts from the wars of independence ① *Tue-Sun 0900-1900 (winter 1000-1800), US$0.50*; there is a restaurant opposite, *La Posada del Viajero* (recommended). On the inland side of Route 9, the strange and gloomy Laguna Negra and the marshes of the Bañado de Santa Teresa support large numbers of wild birds. A road encircles the fortress; it's possible to drive or walk around even after closing. From there is a good view of Laguna Negra.

There are countless campsites (open all year), and a few cottages to let in the summer (usually snapped up quickly). At the *capatacia*, or administrative headquarters, campers pay US$4 pp per night. Here there are also a small supermarket, greengrocer, butcher, bakery, medical clinic, petrol station, auto mechanic, post and telephone offices, and the *Club Santa Teresa*, where drinks and meals are available, but expensive. Practically every amenity is closed off-season. The bathing resort of **La Coronilla** is 10 km north of Santa Teresa, 20 south of Chuy; it has several hotels and restaurants, most closed in winter (tourist information T098-169204). Montevideo-Chuy buses stop at La Coronilla.

Chuy → *Phone code: 0474. Population: 10,400.*

At Chuy, 340 km from Montevideo, the Brazilian frontier runs along the main street, Avenida Internacional, which is called Avenida Brasil in Uruguay and Avenida Uruguaí in Brasil. The Uruguayan side has more services, including supermarkets, duty-free shops and a casino.

On the Uruguyan side, on a promontory overlooking Laguna Merín and the gaúcho landscape of southern Brazil, stands the restored fortress of **San Miguel** ① *US$0.75, bus from Chuy US$1.50, Rutas del Sol buses from Montevideo go here after passing through Chuy*, dating from 1734 and surrounded by a moat. It is set above a 1500-ha wetland park, which is good for birdwatching and is 10 km north of Chuy along Route 19 which is the border. There is a small museum of *criollo* and *indígena* culture, displaying, among other artefacts, old carriages and presses. Not always open in low season. A fine walk from here is 2 km to the Cerro Picudo. The path starts behind the museum, very apparent. Tours (US$10 from Chuy) end for the season after 31 March.

Border with Brazil

Uruguayan passport control is 2½ km before the border on Ruta 9 into Chuy, US$2 by taxi, 20 minutes' walk, or take a town bus; officials friendly and cooperative. Ministry of Tourism kiosk here is helpful, especially for motorists, T4599. Tourists may freely cross the border in either direction as long as they do not go beyond either country's border post. Taking a car into Brazil is no problem if the car is not registered in Brazil or Uruguay. (Uruguayan rental cars are not allowed out of the country. Although you can freely drive between Chuy and Chuí, if you break down/have an accident on the Brazilian side, car rental insurance will not cover it: park in Chuy, even if only one metre from Brazil, and walk.) From the border post, Ruta 9 bypasses the town, becoming BR-471 on the Brazilian side, leading to Brazilian immigration, also outside town. The Brazilian consulate is at Tito Fernández 147 esq Samuel Priliac, T2049, Chuy. For buses to Brazilian destinations, go to the rodoviária in Chuí . The bus companies that run from Chuy into Brazil ask for passports – make sure you get yours back before boarding the bus.

Entering Uruguay You need a Brazilian exit stamp and a Uruguayan entry stamp (unless visiting only Chuí), otherwise you'll be turned back at customs or other official posts. Those requiring a visa will be charged around US$80 depending on the country.

East from Montevideo listings

For Sleeping and Eating price codes and other relevant information, see pages 8-9.

🛌 Sleeping

Piriápolis *p45*
Many hotels along the seafront, most close end-Feb to mid-Dec. Book in advance in high season. Many others than those listed here.
$$$ Argentino, Rambla de los Argentinos y Armenia, T22791, www.argentinohotel. com.uy. A fine hotel and landmark designed by Piria with casino, 2 restaurants, medicinal springs, sauna and good facilities for children.
$$$ Centro, Sanabria 931, T22516. With breakfast, cafeteria, helpful about local sites, very near beach.
$$$ Luján, Sanabria 939, T22216. Simple rooms, family run, some rooms have balconies, homeopathist on top floor. Not great value.
$$$ Rivadavia, Rambla de los Argentinos y Trápani, T22532, www.hotelrivadavia.com. Cable TV, mini-bar, open all year (much cheaper in winter).

$ pp Hostel Piriápolis, Simón del Pino 1136 y Tucumán, T20394, www.hostelpiriapolis. com. Rooms for 2-4 (open all year), private rooms **$$**, 240 beds, non-HI members pay more, hot showers, cooking facilities, student cards accepted.
Camping Piriápolis, T23275, on the slope of Cerro del Toro, doubles in bungalows, and tents. Site at Misiones y Niza, just behind bus station, poor showers, smelly toilets, US$5.60.

Portezuelo and Punta Ballena *p46*
$$$$ Casa Pueblo, T578611, www.club hotel.com.ar. Highly recommended hotel and apartments, restaurant, spa and, lower down the hill, a *parrillada*.
$$$$ Hotel-Art Las Cumbres, Ruta 12 Km 3.9, 4 km inland, T578689, www.cumbres. com.uy. Some rooms **$$$** out of season, themed as an artist's house-studio, on a wooded hill with great views over Laguna del Sauce and the coast, pool, restaurant and tea room (expensive but popular).
Campsite Punta Ballena, Km 120, Parada 45, T042-578902, www.campinginternacional

puntaballena.com. US$7 pp per night, many facilities, very clean.

Maldonado *p46*
Hotel accommodation is scarce in summer; cheaper than Punta del Este, but you will have to commute to the beach. Basic 1-2 star places (**$$**), open all year, include: **Catedral**, Florida 830 casi 18 de Julio, T242513, hotelcatedral@adinet.com.uy, central, and **$$$ Colonial**, 18 de Julio 841 y Florida, T223346, www.elhotelcolonial.com.
$$ Hospedaje Isla de Gorriti, Michelini 884, T245218. Nice courtyard. Recommended.
$ Celta, Ituzaingó 839, T/F230139. Helpful, Irish owner, No 7 bus stop outside.
Camping   Parque El Placer, T270034, free.

Punta del Este *p48*
Note   Streets on the peninsula have names and numbers; lowest numbers at the tip. Hotels are plentiful but expensive: we list recommended ones only. Rates in the few hotels still open after the end of Mar are often halved. Visitors without a car have to take a hotel on the peninsula, unless they want to spend a fortune on taxis.

On the peninsula
$$$$ Conrad Hotel y Casino, Parada 4, Playa Mansa, T491111, www.conrad.com.uy. Luxurious hotel with spa, concerts and events, wonderful views. Book in advance in high season.
$$$$ Iberia, C 24, No 685, T440405, iberiapunta@hotmail.com. **$$$** out of season, breakfast included, open all year, garage opposite.
$$$$ Remanso, C 20 y 28, T447412, www.hotelremanso.com.uy. Some rooms **$$$** low season, comfortable, businesslike, pool, safe, open all year (also more expensive suites). Recommended.
$$$ Gaudi, C Risso, parada 1, by bus terminal, T494116, www.hotelgaudi.com.uy.

2-star. Good, a/c, convenient, safe, fridge, Wi-Fi, bar, open all year.
$$$ Palace, Av Gorlero esq 11, T229596, on www.reservas.net click on Punta del Este (closed in winter). 3-star. Breakfast only (expensive restaurant, *La Stampa*, in the hotel), well kept.
$$$ Tánger, C 31 entre 18 y 20, T441333, www.hoteltanger.com. Open all year, a/c, safe, disabled access, 2 pools.
$$ pp Alicia Lorenzo, Parada 5, T480781. Bed and breakfast room with bath, barbecue.
$$ pp Youth hostel 1949, C 30 y 18, T440719, www.1949hostel.com. 100 m from bus station. Small, **$$$** in double (in low season only, **$$**), kitchen, bar, TV and DVD, close to beaches.
$ pp Punta del Este Hostel, C 25 No 544 y 24, T441632, www.puntadelestehostel.com. US$17-25 in dorm (price depends on season; no doubles), includes breakfast, lockers, central, basic.

Beaches east of Punta del Este *p47*
San Rafael (Parada 12)
$$$$ San Marcos, Av Mar del Plata 191, T482 251, www.hotelsanmarcos.com. Pool (covered in winter), prices fall to **$$$** in mid and low season, restaurant, bicycle hire, free internet, very pleasant.
$$$$ San Rafael, Lorenzo Batlle y Pacheco, Parada 11 Brava, T482161, www.hotelsan rafael.com.uy. Large hotel, open all year, suites cost **$$$$** in high season, a/c, heating, safe, TV, spa.
$$$ La Capilla, Viña del Mar y Valparaíso, behind San Marcos, T484059, www.lacapilla. com.uy. Open all year (doubles **$$$$** at Christmas), includes breakfast, kitchenette in some rooms, safes in rooms, gardens, pool, good, recently upgraded.

La Barra
$$$$ Hostal de la Barra, Ruta 10, Km 161.300, T771521, www.hostaldelabarra.net. A small

hotel, not a hostel, with sea view, forest view and loft rooms, open all year, neat, Christmas, Carnival and Semana Santa require 7 or 4-night minimum stays.

$$$$ La Ballenera Bed and Breakfast, Km 162, just off coast road ½ km east of the hilly promontory, behind Playa Montoya, T771079, www.laballenera.com. Half price in low season, big old wooden mansion, lovely breakfast terrace, kitchen and internet.

$$$$ La Posta del Cangrejo, hotel/restaurant, Ruta 10 Km 160, T770021, www.lapostadel cangrejo.com. Nice location, smart, if a bit old. Recommended.

$$$ Mantra, Ruta 10, Parada 48, T771000, www.mantraresort.com. Very good, but you will need a car to move around. Open all year, great pool, casino, restaurants, concerts, own cinema and wine bar. Recommended.

$ pp Backpacker de La Barra, C 9, No 2306, ½ km off main road, T772272, www.backpackerdelabarra.com. Closed in low season (except if large group), youth hostel style, price depends on dates and class of room, 6 night package over New Year, café and restaurant, internet, laundry.

Camping Camping San Rafael, www.campingsanrafael.com.uy. Good facilities, US$12, bus 5 from Maldonado.

Faro José Ignacio

$$$$ Posada del Faro, C de la Bahía y Timonel, T0486-2110, www.posadadel faro.com. Exclusive hotel overlooking the sea, 12 rooms in 4 standards, internet, pool, bar, restaurant, often quoted as the best of the new developments.

Manantiales

Resorts include: **$$$$ Las Dunas**, Ruta 10, Km 163, T771211, hlasdunas@adinet.com.uy, 5-star, opulent (**$$$** in low season), and **$$$$ Las Olas**, Ruta 10, Km 162.5, T770466, www.lasolasresort.com.uy, 4-star.

$$ El Viajero Manantiales, Ruta 10, Km 164, T774427, www.manantialeshostel.com. **$** in dorm. HI affiliated. Swimming pool, kitchen, bikes and surfboards for rent, lockers, DVDs, laundry, Wi-Fi, bar, open Nov to Apr.

La Paloma *p48*

$$$ Bahía, Av del Navío s/n, entre Solari y Del Sol, T6029, www.elbahia.com.uy. Breakfast, rooms for 2-4, clean and simple, quite old-fashioned, TV, Wi-Fi, laundry.

$$$ Embeleco, Virgen y Sol, T6108. Breakfast, half price in winter, welcoming. 1 block from the beach.

$$$ Palma de Mallorca, on Playa La Aguada, in nearby La Aguada, luxury hotel, T6739, www.hotelpalmademallorca.com. Right on the ocean. Discounts for longer stays, heated pool.

$ pp Reserva Ecológica La Laguna, 2 km north of Aguas Dulces, T0475-2118/099-602410, http://lalagunauruguay.spaces. live.com/. Rustic cabins on the shore a lake, price depends on number of occupants, also day rates (US$55 adults, US$35 children), full and half-board available, close to beach, horse riding, trekking, sailing, hydrobikes, meditation. Always phone in advance for directions and reservation.

Youth hostels $ pp Altena 5000 at Parque Andresito, T6396, www.lapaloma hostel.com. 50 beds, HI discounts, clean, friendly, good meals, kitchen, open all year. Also **$ pp Ibirapita**, Av Paloma s/n, 250 m from bus station, 200 m from beach, T9303, www.hostelibirapita.com. Cheaper in mixed dorm and for HI members, doubles **$$**. Buffet breakfast, Wi-Fi, surf boards, bicycles.

Camping In **Parque Andresito**, T6081. Overpriced, thatched *cabañas* for rent, US$50 per day with maid and kitchen facilities, sleep 4-6. *Grill del Camping* for *parrillas*. **La Aguada**, T6239, 1 km east of town, 300 m from beach, US$5-6. Good, each site with BBQ, tap, sink, water and electricity.

Northeast of La Paloma

At **Cabo Polonio** you cannot camp. There are posadas, some listed below, or you can rent a house; see **www.cabopolonio.com** or **www.portaldelcabo.com.uy** for all options. Water is drawn from wells (*cachimba*) and there is no electricity (some houses have generators, some gas lamps, otherwise buy candles). There are 4 shops for supplies, largest is **El Templao**. At **Aguas Dulces** there are various places to stay and lots of cheap cabins for rent.

$$$ La Pedrera, La Pedrera, T0479-2001, hpedrera@adinet.com.uy. 2 pools, tennis court, restaurant, good rooms.

$$$ La Perla, Cabo Polonio, T0470-5125, T099-871017, www.mayoral.com.uy/. Meals US$8-11. Rooms to rent; no credit cards, horse riding, visits to lighthouse, open all year.

$$$ Mariemar, Cabo Polonio, T0470-5164, 099-875260, mariemar@cabopolonio.com. Nice owners, own electricity generator, hot water, with breakfast, restaurant, open all year. Recommended.

$$$ Posada Eirete, Barra de Valizas, T0475-4011, www.posadaeiretevalizas.com. Small, tasteful, good breakfasts, owned by painter María Beloso. Highly recommended.

$ pp Cabo Polonio Hostel, T099-445 943, www.cabopoloniohostel.com. Small wooden hostel, hot showers, shared rooms but doubles outside high season (**$$**), kitchenettes, solar power, bar, good fresh food, can arrange tours and riding.

$ pp La Cañada, about 1 km outside Cabo Polonio, T099-550595, posadalacaniada@cabopolonio.com. Shared rooms and a few doubles, friendly, small restaurant. They also rent out a cabin.

Reserva Ecológica La Laguna, about 2 km from Aguas Dulces, T099-602410/0475-2118. Private reserve on a 25 ha lake, with cabins for 4-6 (**$ pp**), meals extra, open all year, many languages spoken, pick-up from bus stop in jeep, tours arranged, activities. (Rutas del Sol bus from Montevideo, US$10).

Youth hostels At La Pedrera: **El Viajero**, 500 m from beach, T0479-2252, www.la pedrerahostel.com. Open mid-Nov to 31 Mar, US$26-42 in double with bath, US$16-27 in dorm, kitchen, internet, surf classes, riding. **La Duna**, Carretero 685, Barra de Valizas, T0475-4045, open Dec-Mar, US$14 (HI members) US$18 (non-members), in dorm. Some doubles. Both are HI hostels.

Camping Camping Esmeralda, at Km 280.5, 17 km north of Castillos. **La Palomita**, 8 blocks from the sea, La Pedrera. Wooded, electricity, US$5, summer only.

Punta del Diablo *p49*

In high season you should book in advance; www.portaldeldiablo.com gives a full list of choices.

$$$$ Aquarella, Av No 5, ½ block from beach, T0477-2400, www.portaldel diablo.com. Pool, jacuzzi, great views, restaurant in high season.

$$$ Posada Rocamar, Calle 5 No 3302, T0477-2516, www.posadarocamar.com.uy. Doubles and family suites, tastefully decorated, outdoor patio, peaceful, excursions to Laguna Negra organized.

$ pp El Diablo Tranquilo Hostel and Bar, Av Central, T0477-2647, www.eldiablo tranquilo.com, shared and private rooms, double suites with fireplaces (**$$**), great internet access, breakfast and cooking facilities, year round. Separate bar that is one of the nightlife hotspots. Highly recommended.

$ Hostería del Pescador, on road into village, Blv Santa Teresa, T0477-2017, www.portaldel diablo.com. Rooms for 2-5, price vary for season and day of week, with breakfast, restaurant, pool.

$ Posada de Maite, Calles 11 y 10, T0477-2335, www.portaldeldiablo.com. Rooms for 2-6 people, English spoken, Wi-Fi, BBQ, pool, very nice.

$ pp Punta del Diablo Hostel, Km 298, Ruta 9, T0477-2655, www.puntadeldiablo hostel.com. Discounts for HI members. With kitchen, camping (US$8-10 pp), bicycles, free internet, open end-Dec to end-Feb.

Chuy *p49*
All hotels are open the year round.
$$$ Parador Fortín de San Miguel, Paraje 18 de Julio, near San Miguel fortress, T6607, www.elfortin.com. Excellent, full and half-board, colonial-style hotel. Beautiful rooms, gym, pool, fine food and service. Highly recommended. You don't have to go through Uruguayan formalities to get there from Brazil.
$$ Alerces, Laguna de Castillos 578, T2260, alerces@montevideo.com.uy. 4 blocks from border. Bath, TV, breakfast, heater, pool.
$$ Nuevo Hotel Plaza, C Artigas y Av Arachanes, T2309, www.hotelplaza.chuynet.com. On plaza, bath, good buffet breakfast, TV, very helpful, good, restaurant *El Mesón del Plaza*.
$$ Vittoria, Numancia 143, T2280. Price includes breakfast, simple and clean, parking.
Camping From Chuy buses run every 2 hrs to the Barra del Chuy campsite, Ruta 9 Km 331, turn right 13 km, T2425. Good bathing, many birds. *Cabañas* for up to 4 persons cost US$20 daily or less, depending on amenities.

🍴 Eating

Portezuelo and Punta Ballena *p46*
$$$ Medio y Medio, Cont Camino Lussich s/n, Punta Ballena, T578791, www.medioy medio.com. Jazz club and restaurant, music nightly and good food.
$$$-$$ Las Vertientes, Camino de Los Ceibos, 2 km on the Route 9, T042-669997. Country restaurant, fresh food which all comes from own farm, good salads and sweets.

Maldonado *p46*
Best ice cream at **Popy's**.
$$$-$$ Lo de Rubén, Florida y Santa Teresa, T223059. Open every day. *Parrillada*, best restaurant in town.

$$$-$$ Taberna Patxi, Dodera 944, T238393. Very good Basque food with authentic recipes.

Punta del Este *p46, map p48*
Many enticing ice cream parlours on Gorlero.
$$$ Bungalow Suizo, Av Roosevelt y Parada 8, T482358. Excellent Swiss, must book.
$$$ Cantón Chino, Calle 28 y Gorlero, T441316. Creative Chinese food, good.
$$$ El Ciclista, Calle 20 y 29, T448371. Long-standing, with international cuisine, Italian, *parrilla* and seafood. Recently moved to new building.
$$$ Gure-etxe (also in La Coronilla), Calle 9 y 12, T446858. Seafood and Basque cuisine.
$$$ Isidora, Rambla del Puerto, esq 21, T449646, www.isidora.com.uy. Smart, by the port, international cuisine beautifully presented.
$$$ Juana Enea, Calle 9, No 607, T447236. Restaurant and fishmonger, fresh fish, popular with locals.
$$$ La Bourgogne, Pedragosa Sierra y Av del Mar, T482007. Elegant French/South American cuisine, fresh ingredients, chef Jean-Paul Bondoux.
$$$ Los Caracoles, Calle 20 y 28, T440912. Excellent food (international, *parrilla*, seafood) at good prices.
$$$ Lo de Charlie, Calle 12 y 9, T444183. Fish, including tuna and octopus, plus pasta and *parrilla* standards.
$$$ Lo de Tere, Rambla Artigas y 21, T440492, www.lode tere.com. Good local food, open all year but closed Wed in winter, 20% discount if eating lunch before 1300 or dinner before 2100. Highly recommended.
$$$ Viejo Marino, Calle 11 entre 14 y 12, Las Palmeras, T443565. Fish restaurant, busy, go early.
$$$ Virazón, Rambla Artigas y C 28, T443924. Good food and great view, but expensive. Recommended.
$$$ Yatch Club Uruguayo, Rambla Artigas y 8, T441056. Very good, fish, seafood, views

over the port (not to be confused with the Yacht Club).

$$ Il Barreto, C 9 y 10, T446916. Italian vegetarian, good value, live Italian and Latin music some evenings, in low season open weekends only.

Beaches east of Punta del Este p47
La Barra

$$$ Baby Gouda Café, Ruta 10, Km 161, T771874. Alternative food, yoga and Arab dances.

$$$-$$ Restaurant T, Ruta 10, Km 49.5, T771356. Old-style, Italian and French as well as local dishes, good wine selection. Claims to be the only "real" bistro in Punta del Este

Faro José Ignacio

$$$ La Huella, Los Cisnes on Playa Brava, T0486-2279. Excellent seafood, on the beach.
$$$ Marismo, Ruta 10 Km185, T0486-2273. Romantic, outdoor tables around a fire.

Manantiales

$$$ Cactus y Pescados, Primera Bajada a Bikini, T774782. Very good seafood, international menu.

La Paloma p48

$$$ La Marea, Av Solari, near tourist office. Very popular, has outstanding seafood.
$$ Arrecife, Av Principal, T0479-6837. First class, serving pizzas, *parrilla* and a good range of salads.
$$ Da Carlos, Av Solari. Moderate prices, pizzas plus Uruguayan food.

Northeast of La Paloma

In **Cabo Polonio**, there are a few restaurants, some with vegetarian options, so you don't have to bring any food with you. Fish is on the menu when the sea is calm enough for the fishermen to go out. The most expensive and fashionable is **La Puesta**, on the south beach. On weekends during the summer there are DJs, dancing and live music. For self-catering,

the stores sell fruit, vegetables, meat, etc. There are several restaurants in **Castillos** including RRR **La Strada**, 19 de Abril, and several restaurants in **Punta del Diablo**, mostly colourful huts grouped around the sea front serving excellent fish. A couple of pizza places too.

$$ Chivito Veloz, Aguas Dulces. Good, large portions for US$5.

Parque Nacional Santa Teresa p49

$$ La Ruta, La Coronilla. This small round restaurant at the entrance to town may be your only option if you are driving in the evening and off season from Chuy to Punta or Montevideo. Good meat dishes. Off season, other restaurants in Coronilla are closed.

Chuy p49

$$-$ Fusion, Av Brasil 387. Good food, not traditional Uruguayan fare. Recommended
$$-$ Restaurant Jesús, Av Brasil y L Olivera. Good value and quality.

🎵 Bars and clubs

Punta del Este p46, map p48
Hop, Rambla Artigas, T446061, www.hop.com.uy. Bar and restaurant, popular drinking spot.
Moby Dick, Rambla del Puerto. Mock English-style pub by the port, open until the early hours, very popular.
Ocean Club, Parada 12 de la Brava, T484869, www.oceanclub.com.uy. Very fashionable and smart club playing mostly pop and house. Dress up.

⛰️ Activities and tours

Punta del Este p46, map p48
Diving Punta Divers, C 32, No 626, T482481, www.ssila.com. US$290 for 8 dives to caves at Punta Ballena and Gorriti, and to wrecks (eg HMS *Agamemon*, Nelson's favourite ship), courses offered. Trips include refreshments. Also offer dive in a gold mine near Minas. To see right whales at end-Aug to Nov, US$18.

Riding Nueva Escuela de Equitación, at Cantegril Country Club, Av Saravia, T223211. Classes, guided rides for all levels and ages.

⊖ Transport

Piriápolis *p45*

Road Piriápolis may be reached either by following the very beautiful R10 from the end of the Interbalnearia, or by taking the original access road (R37) from Pan de Azúcar, which crosses the R93. The shortest route from Piriápolis to Punta del Este is by the Camino de las Bases which runs parallel to the R37 and joins the R93 some 4 km east of the R37 junction.

Bus Terminal on Misiones, 2 blocks from Hotel Argentino, T24141. To/from **Montevideo**, US$5, 1½ hrs. To **Punta del Este**, US$4, 50 mins. To **Maldonado**, US$3, 40 mins. For **Rocha**, **La Paloma** and **Chuy**, take bus to Pan de Azúcar and change.

Maldonado *p46*

Bus Av Roosevelt y Sarandí. To/from **Montevideo**, US$7; to **Minas**, 2 hrs, 5 a day, US$4.50. To **San Carlos** take a local bus 3 blocks from the main bus station, US$1.50.

Punta del Este *p46, map p48*

Air Direct daily Boeing 737 flights from Buenos Aires to brand new Punta del Este airport during the high season. **Laguna del Sauce**, Capitán Curbelo (T559777), which handles flights to Buenos Aires, 40 mins. Airport tax US$30. Exchange facilities, tax-free shopping. Regular bus service to airport from Punta del Este (will deliver to and collect from private addresses and hotels), US$5, 90 mins before departure, also connects with arriving flights. Taxi US$25; *remise* around US$30 depending on destination (T441269). El Jagüel airport is used by private planes.

Bus **Local**: Traffic is directed by a one-way system; town bus services start from C 5 (El Faro), near the lighthouse. www.puntaweb.com has details of bus routes. **Long distance**: terminal at Av Gorlero, Blvd Artigas and C 32, T486810 (served by local bus No 7); has toilets, newsagent, café and Casa de Cambio. To/from **Montevideo** via Carrasco airport, **COT** (T486810) or **Copsa** (T1975), US$7.50, just over 2 hrs, many in the summer; 19 a day in winter. To **Piriápolis**, US$4. To **San Carlos** (US$1.50) for connections to Porto Alegre, Rocha, La Paloma, Chuy. Direct to **Chuy**, 4 hrs, US$12. Local bus fare about US$0.50. For transport Montevideo-Buenos Aires, **Buquebus** T488380, at bus terminal, loc 09, buses connect with ferries. Also **Colonia Express**.

La Paloma *p48*

Bus Frequent to and from **Rocha**, US$1.75, and to and from **the capital** (5 hrs, US$12). 4 buses daily to **Chuy**, US$8, 3½ hrs, 2 a day to San Carlos, Pan de Azúcar and Aguas Dulces, all with **Rutas del Sol**. Northeast of La Paloma, some Montevideo-Chuy buses go into **Punta del Diablo**, 4 km from the main road.

To **Cabo Polonio**, Rutas del Sol from Montevideo, US$15, 4-5 hrs, and any of the coastal towns to Km 264, where you catch the truck to the village (see above).

Chuy *p49*

Bus To **Montevideo** (COT, Cynsa, Rutas del Sol) US$17, 4¾-6 hrs, may have to change buses in San Carlos; to **Maldonado** US$7.50. International buses passing through en route from Montevideo to Brazil either stop in Chuy or at the border. Make sure the driver knows you need to stop at Uruguayan immigration. Sometimes everybody must get off for customs check. If looking for onward transport, if there is a free seat, most companies will let you pay on board.

Piriápolis *p45*
Banks BROU on Rambla Argentinos changes TCs; **Casa de Cambio Monex**, Argentinos s/n, T25295. **Post office** Av Piria y Tucumán.

Maldonado *p46*
Banks Banco Pan de Azúcar, accepts MasterCard. **Cambio Bacacay**, Florida 803, good rates, TCs.

Punta del Este *p46, map p48*
Airline offices Aerolíneas Argentinas, Edif Edmos Dumont, Av Gorlero, T444343. **Pluna**, Av Roosevelt y Parada 9, T492050/ 490101. **Banks** Best rates of exchange from Banco de la República Oriental de Uruguay, which opens earlier and closes later than the other banks and accepts MasterCard, but no TCs. Many ATMs at banks on the peninsula and at Punta Shopping (Roosevelt). Also *casas de cambio*, eg **Indumex**, Av Gorlero y 28, **Brimar**, C 31 No 610. **Car hire** Punta Car, Continuación Gorlero s/n, Hotel Playa, T482112, puntacar@puntacar.com.uy. **Uno**, Gorlero y 21, T445018, unonobat@ movinet.com.uy. And others. See Essentials, for international agencies. **Internet** Locutorio, Gorlero y 30, T441807, US$2 per hr. Another internet café in **Devoto** shopping centre, Av Roosevelt y Parada 10, T494992. **Post offices** Av Gorlero entre 31 y 32,

0900-1400, 1600-1900, daily (shorter hours out of season). **Scooter hire** US$51 per day, with drivers licence (US$50 fine if caught without it) and ID documents from **Filibusteros**, Av Artigas y Parada 5, T484125. They also rent out bicycles (US$3.50 per hr, US$7.50 per half day, US$10 per day, includes padlocks). **Telephones** Telephone on Calle 24 at Calle 25, by the plaza.

La Paloma *p48*
Internet Arrecife, Av Solari, US$2 per hr, open 1000-0100. **Useful services** Bike rental from **El Tobo**, T0479-7881, US$3.50 a day. One bank which changes TCs; also a supermarket and post office.

Chuy *p49*
Banks Several *cambios* on Av Brasil, eg **Gales**, Artigas y Brasil, Mon-Fri 0830-1200, 1330-1800, Sat 0830-1200, and in World Trade Center, open 1000-2200; on either side of Gales are Aces and Val. All give similar rates, charging US$1 plus 1% commission on TCs, US$, pesos and reais. On Sun, try the casino, or look for someone on the street outside the *cambios*. BROU, Gen Artigas, changes TCs. No problem spending reais in Chuy or pesos in Chuí. **Internet** MPM, Gen Artigas 163, T4358. **Post office** On Gen Artigas. **Telephones** Antel, S Priliac almost Artigas, open 0700-2300.

Montevideo north to Brazil

Two roads run towards Melo, heart of cattle-ranching country: Route 8 and Route 7, the latter running for most of its length through the Cuchilla Grande, a range of hills with fine views. Route 8 via Minas and Treinta y Tres, is the more important of these two roads to the border and it is completely paved.

Minas and around → *Phone code: 0442. Population: 38,000.*
This picturesque small town, 120 km north of Montevideo, is set in wooded hills. Juan Lavalleja, the leader of the Thirty-Three who brought independence to the country, was born here, and there is an equestrian statue to Artigas, said to be the largest such in the world, on the Cerro Artigas just out of town. The church's portico and towers, some caves in the neighbourhood and the countryside are worth seeing. Good confectionery is made in Minas; you can visit the largest firm, opposite *Hotel Verdun*. Banks are open 1300-1700 Monday-Friday. There is a tourist office at the bus station.

The Parque Salus, on the slopes of Sierras de las Animas, is 8 km to the south and very attractive; take the town bus marked 'Cervecería Salus' from plaza to the Salus brewery, then walk 2 km to the mineral spring and bottling plant (**$$$** *Parador Salus*, good). It is a lovely three-hour walk back to Minas from the springs. The Cascada de Agua del Penitente waterfall, 11 km east off Route 8, is interesting and you may see wild rheas nearby. It's hard to get to off season.

To the Brazilian border
Route 8 continues north via **Treinta y Tres** (*Population: 26,000*) to Melo (also reached by Route 7), near Aceguá close to the border. In **Melo** (*Phone code: 0462; Population: 51,000*), there are places to stay and exchange rates are usually better than at the frontier. If crossing to Brazil here, Brazilian immigration is at Bagé, not at the border. At 12 km southeast of Melo is the Posta del Chuy (2 km off Route 26). This house, bridge and toll gate (built 1851) was once the only safe crossing place on the main road between Uruguay and Brazil. It displays gaucho paintings and historical artefacts.

Río Branco was founded in 1914, on the Río Yaguarón. The 1 km-long Mauá bridge across the river leads to Jaguarão in Brazil. The Brazilian vice-consulate in Río Branco is at Calle Ismael Velázquez 1239, T0675-2003, bravcrb@gmail.com. For road traffic, the frontier at Chuy is better than Río Branco or Aceguá. There is a toll 68 km north of Montevideo.

An alternative route to Brazil is via Route 5, the 509-km road from Montevideo to the border town of Rivera, which runs almost due north, bypassing Canelones and Florida before passing through Durazno. After crossing the Río Negro, it goes to Tacuarembó. South of the Río Negro is gently rolling cattle country, vineyards, orchards, orange, lemon and olive groves. North is hilly countryside with steep river valleys and cattle ranching. The road is dual carriageway as far as Canelones.

East of Florida, Route 56 traverses the countryside eastwards to **Cerro Colorado**, also known as Alejandro Gallinal, which has an unusual clock tower.

Durazno → *Phone code: 0362. Population: 30,700.*
On the Río Yí 182 km from Montevideo, Durazno is a friendly provincial town with tree-lined avenues and an airport. There is a good view of the river from the western bridge.

Dams on the Río Negro have created an extensive network of lakes near **Paso de los Toros** (*Population: 13,000; 66 km north of Durazno, bus from Montevideo US$13*), with camping and sports facilities. Some 43 km north of Paso de los Toros a 55-km road turns east to **San Gregorio de Polanco**, at the eastern end of Lago Rincón del Bonete. The beach by the lake is excellent, with opportunities for boat trips, horse riding and other sports.

Tacuarembó ➔ *Phone code: 063. Population: 51,000.*
This is an agro-industrial town and major route centre 390 km north of Montevideo. The nearby Valle Edén has good walking possibilities. Some 23 km west of Tacuarembó, along Route 26, is the **Carlos Gardel Museum** ① *US$1, daily 0900-1800*, a shrine to the great tango singer who was killed in an air crash in Medellín (Colombia). Uruguay, Argentina and France all claim him as a national son. The argument for his birth near here is convincing.

Brazilian border
Rivera (*Population: 64,400, Phone code: 062*) is divided by a street from the Brazilian town of Santa Ana do Livramento. Points of interest are the park, the Plaza Internacional, and the dam of Cañapirú. Uruguayan immigration is at the end of Calle Sarandí y Presidente Viera, 14 blocks, 2 km, from the border (take bus along Agraciada or taxi from bus terminal for around US$1.50). There is also a tourist office here, T31900. Luggage is inspected when boarding buses out of Rivera; there are also 3 checkpoints on the road out of town. The Brazilian consulate is at Ceballos 1159, T23278. Remember that you must have a Uruguayan exit stamp to enter Brazil and a Brazilian exit stamp to enter Uruguay.

Montevideo north to Brazil listings

For Sleeping and Eating price codes and other relevant information, see pages 8-9.

⊜ Sleeping

Minas *p58*
$$ Posada Verdun, W Beltrán 715, T24563, posadaverdun@hotmail.com. Good, breakfast extra (**Confitería Nuevo Sabor** nearby serves good food).

$ Hostel de Villa Serrana, C Molle s/n off Route 8, Km 145, in Villa Serrana, T09-922 6911, www.villa serranahostel.com. Oldest hostel in Uruguay. US$8 pp, open all year, 28 km beyond Minas on road to Treinta y Tres. Thatched house, kitchen for members, horses for hire, basic, take plenty of food and drink (no shop). Direct bus from Montevideo to Treinta y Tres or Melo, ask to be set down at Km 145 and walk 2 km to Villa Serrana. Or take bus to Minas from Montevideo or Punta

del Este then **Cosu** bus Tue, Thu 0900, 1730 to Villa Serrana.

Camping Arequita, Camino Valeriano Magri, T0440-2503, beautiful surroundings, cabañas (for 2 people with shared bathroom US$12.50), camping US$3 each.

Tourism farm $$$ Posada El Abra, Puntas de Santa Lucía, 25 km from Minas, T0440-2869, www.elabra.com.uy. Small *estancia* in hills at Río Santa Lucía headwaters, full board, includes transport, guides, horses for riding, good walking, swimming in river, expansive views.

To the Brazilian border *p58*
Treinta y Tres
$ pp Cañada del Brujo, Km 307.5, Ruta 8, Sierra del Yerbal, 34 km north of Treinta y Tres, T0452-2837, T099-297448 (mob), cdelbrujo@latinmail.com. Isolated hostel,

no electricity, basic but "fantastic", dorm, local food, owner Pablo Rado drives you there, canoeing, trekking on foot or horseback, trips to Quebrada de los Cuervos. Recommended.
$ La Posada, Manuel Freire 1564, T21107, www.hotellaposada33.com. With breakfast, good overnight stop.

Melo
$$ Virrey Pedro de Melo, J Muñiz 727, T22673, www.hotelvirreypedrodemelo. com. Better rooms in new part, 3-star, TV, minibar, café.

Cerro Colorado
$$$$ San Pedro de Timote, Km 142, R7, 14 km west of Cerro Colorado, T0598-310 8086, http://sanpedrodetimote.com.uy. A famous colonial-style *estancia*, working ranch, landscaped park, 3 pools, cinema, gym, horse riding, good restaurant.
$$$ Arteaga, 7 km off R7 north of Cerro Colorado, T02-707 4766, arteaga@ paradaarteaga.com. Typical European *estancia*, famous, beautiful interior, pool.

Durazno *p58*
There are a few hotels (**$**).
Camping At 33 Orientales, in park of same name by river, T2806, nice beach, hot showers, toilets, laundry sinks.
Tourism Farm Estancia Albergue El Silencio, Ruta 14 Km 166, 10 km west of Durazno, T2014 (or T0360-2270, HI member), www.estancia elsilencio.net. About 15 mins walk east of bridge over Río Yí where bus stops, clean rooms, friendly, riding, swimming, birdwatching. Recommended.

Paso de los Toros
$ Sayonara, Sarandí y Barreto, T0664-2535/2743 2 blocks centre, renovated old residence, rooms with bath, a/c and cable TV. Breakfast extra, US$3.50.

San Gregorio de Polanco
$$ Posada Buena Vista, De Las Pitangueras 12, T0369-4841, www.san-gregorio-de-polanco.com. Overlooking lake, breakfast extra, good.

Tacuarembó *p59*
$$$ Carlos Gardel, Ruta 5 Km 388,500, T30306, www.hotelcarlosgardel.com.uy. Internet, pool, restaurant, meeting room.
$$$ Tacuarembó, 18 de Julio 133, T22104, www.tacuarembohotel.com.uy. Breakfast, central, TV, Wi-Fi, safe, restaurant, pool, parking.
$$ Central, Gral Flores 300, T22841. Cable TV, ensuite bathrooms, rooms with or without a/c, laundry service.
$$ pp **Panagea**, 1 hr from Tacuarembó, T099-836149, http://panagea-uruguay. blogspot. com. Estancia and backpackers' hostel, working cattle and sheep farm, home cooking, lots of riding, electricity till 2200 is only concession to modern amenities, many languages spoken.
Camping Campsites 1 km out of town in the Parque Laguna de las Lavanderas, T4761, and 7 km north on R26 at Balneario Iporá.

Brazilian border: Rivera *p59*
$$ Casablanca, Sarandí 484. Shower, breakfast, a/c, TV, comfortable, pleasant.
$ Sarandí, Sarandí 777, T33963. Fan, good, cheaper without bath.
Camping Municipal site near AFE station, and in the Parque Gran Bretaña 7 km south along R27.

❶ Eating

Minas *p58*
Restaurants include **Complejo San Francisco de las Sierras**, Ruta 12 Km 347,500 (4 km from Minas); **Ki-Joia**, Diego Pérez in front of Plaza Libertad.
Irisarri, C Treinta y Tres 618. Best pastry shop, *yemas* (egg candy) and *damasquitos* (apricot sweets).

Tacuarembó *p59*
Parrilla La Rueda, W Beltrán 251. Good.

Minas *p58*
Bus To **Montevideo**, US$8, 5 companies,
2 hrs. To **Maldonado**, US$4.50, 7 a day,
1½ hrs (**COOM**).

To the Brazilian border: Melo *p58*
Bus To **Montevideo** US$21, 5 hrs
(**Cota, Núñez, Turismar**). Several buses
daily to Río Branco.

Durazno *p58*
Bus To **Montevideo** US$9.50, 2½ hrs.

Tacuarembó *p59*
Bus From **Montevideo**, US$19.50, 4-5 hrs.

Brazilian border: Rivera *p59*
Bus Terminal at Uruguay y Viera (1½ km
from the terminal in Santa Ana). To/from
Montevideo, US$25, 5½-6¾ hrs (**Agencia
Central, Turil, Núñez**). To **Paysandú**,
Copay, T23733, at 0400, 1600, US$18.
To **Tacuarembó**, US$5.50 (**Núñez, Turil**),
no connections for Paysandú. To **Salto**,
Mon and Fri 1630, 6 hrs, US$20. For
Artigas, take bus from Livramento to
Quaraí, then cross bridge.

Contents

At a glance

⟳ **Time required** 1-2 weeks.

❀ **Best time** Sep-Nov, Mar-May.

✖ **When not to go** Holiday season, Jan-Feb, is very crowded.

Buenos Aires

Buenos Aires

With its elegant architecture and fashion-conscious inhabitants, Buenos Aires is often seen as more European than South American. Among its fine boulevards, neat plazas, parks, museums and theatres, there are chic shops and superb restaurants. However, the enormous steaks and passionate tango are distinctly Argentine, and to really understand the country, you have to know its capital. South and west of Buenos Aires the flat, fertile lands of the pampa húmeda stretch seemingly without end, the horizon broken only by a lonely windpump or a line of poplar trees. This is home to the gaucho, whose traditions of music and craftsmanship remain alive.

Ins and outs → *Phone code: 011. Population: 2.78 million (Greater Buenos Aires 12.05 million).*
Getting there Buenos Aires has two **airports**, Ezeiza, for international flights, and Aeroparque, for domestic flights and most services to Uruguay. Ezeiza is 35 km southwest of the centre by a good dual carriageway which links with the General Paz highway which circles the city. The safest way between airport and city is by an airport bus service run every 30 minutes by *Manuel Tienda León*, which has convenient offices and charges US$11 one way. Radio taxis (such as *Onda Verde*, T4867 0000) charge US$32 (plus US$1.20 toll). *Remise* taxis (booked in advance) charge US$32 (including toll for a return journey) airport to town. Aeroparque is 4 km north of the city centre on the riverside; *Manuel Tienda León* has buses between the airports and also runs from Aeroparque to the centre for US$6. Remises charge US$8 and ordinary taxis US$6. As well as by air, travellers from Uruguay arrive by ferry (fast catamaran or slower vessels), docking in the port in the heart of the city, or by bus. All international and interprovincial buses use the Retiro **bus terminal** at Ramos Mejía y Antártida Argentina, which is next to the Retiro railway station. Both are served by city buses, taxis and Line C of the Subte (metro). Other train services, to the province of Buenos Aires and the suburbs use Constitución, Once and Federico Lacroze stations, all served by bus, taxi and Subte. ▶▶ *See also Transport, page 90.*

Getting around The commercial heart of the city, from Retiro station and Plaza San Martín through Plaza de Mayo to San Telmo, east of Avenida 9 de Julio, can be explored on foot, but you'll probably want to take a couple of days to explore its museums, shops and markets. Many places of interest lie outside this zone, so you will need to use public transport. City **buses** (*colectivos*) are plentiful. The fare is about US$0.30 in the city, US$0.50 to the suburbs. The **metro**, or Subte, is fast and clean. It has six lines; a single fare is US$0.30. Yellow and black **taxis** can be hailed on the street, but if at all possible, book a radio taxi by phone as it is much safer s(make sure the meter is reset when you get in). *Remise* taxis, booked only through an office, cost more but are the most reliable. See Transport, below, for full details. Street numbers start from the dock side rising from east to west, but north/ south streets are numbered from Avenida Rivadavia, one block north of Avenida de Mayo rising in both directions. Calle Juan D Perón used to be called Cangallo, and Scalabrini Ortiz used to be Canning (old names are still referred to). Avenida Roque Sáenz Peña and Avenida Julio A Roca are commonly referred to as Diagonal Norte and Diagonal Sur respectively.

Tourist offices National office ⓘ *Av Santa Fe 883, T4312 2232, info@turismo.gov.ar, Mon-Fri 0900-1700*, maps and literature covering the whole country. There are kiosks at Aeroparque (*Aerolíneas Argentinas* section), and at **Ezeiza Airport** daily 0800-2000. **City information** ⓘ *municipal website www.bue.gov.ar, in Spanish, English and Portuguese*. There are tourist kiosks at Florida 100, at the junction of Florida and Marcelo T de Alvear (Monday-Friday 1000-1800), in Recoleta (Av Quintana 596, junction with Ortiz), in Puerto Madero (Dock 4, T4315 4265, 0930-1930, also has information on Montevideo), and at Retiro Bus Station (ground floor, T4313 0187, 0730-1430). Free guided tours are organized by the city authorities: free leaflet from city-run offices and suggested circuits on www.bue.gov.ar. Audio guided tours in several languages are available for 12 itineraries by downloading MP3 files from www.bue.gov.ar, or by dialing *8283 from a mobile phone (look for the grey plaques on the pavement showing a code in many sites around the city). **Tango information centre** ⓘ *on the first floor of Galerías Pacífico, Sarmiento 1551, T4373 2823*. Those overcharged or cheated can go to the **Tourist Ombudsman** ⓘ *Av Pedro de Mendoza 1835 (Museo Quinquela Martín, La Boca), T4302 7816, turista@defensoria.org.ar, and Defensa 1250, T4046 9682, turistasantelmo@defensoría.org.ar, both daily 1000-1800*, or to **Defensa del Consumidor** ⓘ *Venezuela 842, T4338 4900, Mon-Fri 1000-1800*.

South American Explorers has had an office in Buenos Aires for several years, a comfortable meeting place for travellers and source of knowledgeable advice. In May 2010, a new clubhouse opened at Chile 557, San Telmo. See www.saexplorers.org/ clubhouses/ buenosaires for latest information.

Information Good guides to bus and subway routes are **Guía T**, **Lumi**, **Peuser** and **Filcar** (covering the city and Greater Buenos Aires in separate editions), US$1-9 available at news stands. Also handy is Auto Mapa's pocket-size **Plano** of the Federal Capital, or the more detailed City Map covering La Boca to Palermo, both available at news stands, US$4.50; otherwise it is easy to get free maps of the centre from tourist kiosks and most hotels. **Buenos Aires Day & Night** is one of several free bi-monthly tourist magazines with useful information and a downtown map available at tourist kiosks and hotels. *Bainsider* (www.ba insidermag.com) is a fantastic magazine for getting to know the city. **La Nación** (www.lanacion.com.ar) has a very informative Sunday tourism section. On Friday, the youth section of **Clarín** (*Sí*) lists free entertainment; also see www.clarin.com. **Página 12** has a youth supplement on Thursday called **NO**. The **Buenos Aires Herald** publishes **Get Out** on Friday, listing entertainments. Information on what's on at www.buenosairesherald.com.

Other websites worth exploring: www.whatsupbuenosaires.com for detailed lsitings in English; the blogs, www.baexpats.com, www.baires.elsur.org, www.goodmorningba.com, and the video site www.scoopingargentina.com.

Sights

The capital has been virtually rebuilt since the beginning of the 20th-century and its oldest buildings mostly date from the early 1900s, with some elegant examples from the 1920s and 1930s. The centre has maintained the original layout since its foundation and so the streets are often narrow and mostly one way. Its original name, 'Santa María del Buen Ayre' was a recognition of the good winds which brought sailors across the ocean.

Around Plaza de Mayo

The heart of the city is the **Plaza de Mayo**. On the east side is the **Casa de Gobierno**. Called the *Casa Rosada* because it is pink, it contains the offices of the President of the Republic. It is notable for its statuary and the rich furnishing of its halls. The **Museo de los Presidentes** ① *in the basement of the same building, T4344 3804, www.museo.gov.ar, closed in 2010, take passport*, has historical memorabilia. Behind the building, in the semicircular Parque Colón, is a large statue of Columbus. **Antiguo Congreso Nacional** (Old Congress Hall, 1864-1905) ① *Balcarce 139, Thu, 1500-1700, closed Jan-Feb, free*, on the south of the Plaza, is a National Monument. The **Cathedral**, on the north of Plaza, stands on the site of the first church in Buenos Aires ① *Rivadavia 437, T4331 2845, Mon-Fri 0800-1900, Sat-Sun 0900-1930; for guided visits, Mon-Fri 1130 (San Martín's mausoleum and Crypt), 1315 (religious art), daily 1530 (Temple and Crypt); Jan-Feb: Mon-Fri 1100 both Temple and Crypt; mass is held daily, check times*. The current structure dates from 1753-1822 (its portico built in 1827), but the 18th-century towers were never rebuilt, so that the architectural proportions have suffered. The imposing tomb (1880) of the Liberator, Gen José de San Martín, is guarded by soldiers in fancy uniforms. **Museo del Cabildo y la Revolución de Mayo** ① *T4334 1782, Tue-Fri 1030-1700, Sun 1130-1800, US$1; guided visits Sun 1230, 1530, US$1.20* is in the old Cabildo where the movement for independence from Spain was first planned. It's worth a visit for the paintings of old Buenos Aires, the documents and maps recording the May 1810 revolution, and memorabilia of the 1806 British attack; also Jesuit art. In the patio is a café and stalls selling handicrafts (Thursday-Friday 1100-1800). Also on the Plaza is the Palacio de Gobierno de la Ciudad (City Hall). Within a few blocks north of the Plaza are the main banks and business houses, such as the **Banco de la Nación**, opposite the Casa Rosada, with an impressively huge main hall and topped by a massive marble dome 50 m in diameter.

On the Plaza de Mayo, the **Mothers and Grandmothers of the Plaza de Mayo** march in remembrance of their children who disappeared during the 'dirty war' of the 1970s (their addresses are H Yrigoyen 1584, T4383 0377, www.madres.org, and Piedras 153, T4343 1926, www.madresfundadoras.org.ar). The Mothers march anti-clockwise round the central monument every Thursday at 1530, with photos of their disappeared loved-ones pinned to their chests.

West of Plaza de Mayo

Running west from the Plaza, the Avenida de Mayo leads 1½ km to the **Palacio del Congreso** (Congress Hall) ① *Plaza del Congreso, T4953 3081, ext 3885 for guided visits, Mon, Tue, Thu, Fri 1100, 1700, 1900, www.congreso.gov.ar; passport essential*. This huge Greco-Roman building houses the seat of the legislature. Avenida de Mayo has several examples of fine architecture of the early 20th-century, such as the sumptuous La Prensa building (No 575, free guided visits at weekends), the traditional *Café Tortoni* (No 825, www.cafetortoni.com.ar), or the eclectic Palacio Barolo (No 1370, www.pbarolo.com.ar), and many others of faded grandeur. Avenida de Mayo crosses the **Avenida 9 de Julio**, one of the widest avenues in the world, which consists of three major carriageways with heavy traffic, separated in some parts by wide grass borders. Five blocks north of Avenida de Mayo the great **Plaza de la República**, with a 67-m obelisk commemorating the 400th anniversary of the city's founding, is at the junction of Avenida 9 de Julio with Avenidas Roque Sáenz Peña and Corrientes. **Teatro Colón** ① *entrance on Libertad, between Tucumán and Viamonte, T4378 7132, www.teatrocolon.org.ar*, is one of the world's great opera houses. The interior is resplendent with red plush and gilt; the stage is huge, and salons, dressing rooms and banquet halls are equally sumptuous. A full building restoration is due to be finished in 2010. Check at the website for details of alternative venues and tickets.

Close by is the **Museo del Teatro Nacional Cervantes** ① *Córdoba 1199, T4815 8881, Mon-Fri 1000-1800, free* displays history of the theatre in Argentina and its theatre stages performances. **Museo Judío** ① *Libertad 769, T4123 0102; for visits make an appointment with the rabbi (take identification)*, has religious objects relating to Jewish presence in Argentina in a 19th-century synagogue. Close by is **Museo del Holocausto** (Shoah Museum) ① *Montevideo 919, T4811 3588, www.fmh.org.ar, Mon-Thu 1100-1900, Fri 1100-1600, US$1 (ID required)*, a permanent exhibition of pictures, personal and religious items with texts in Spanish on the Holocaust, antisemitism in Argentina and the lives of many Argentine Jews in the pre- and post-war periods. There are also seminars, temporary art exhibitions and a library (open in the afternoon). **La Chacarita** ① *Guzmán 670, daily 0700-1800, take Subte Line B to the Federico Lacroze station*. This well known cemetery has the lovingly tended tomb of Carlos Gardel, the tango singer.

North of Plaza de Mayo

The city's traditional shopping centre, Calle Florida, is reserved for pedestrians, with clothes and souvenir shops, restaurants and the elegant Galerías Pacífico. More shops are to be found on Avenida Santa Fe, which crosses Florida at Plaza San Martín. Avenida Corrientes, a street of theatres, bookshops, restaurants and cafés, and nearby Calle Lavalle (partly reserved for pedestrians), used to be the entertainment centre, but both are now regarded as faded. Recoleta, Palermo and Puerto Madero have become much more fashionable (see below). The **Basílica Nuestra Señora de La Merced** *J D Perón y Reconquista 207, Mon-Fri 0800-1800*, founded 1604, rebuilt for the third time in the 18th century, has a beautiful interior with baroque and rococo features. In 1807 it was a command post against the invading British. Next door is the **Convento de San Ramón. Museo y Biblioteca Mitre** ① *San Martín 336, T4394 8240, Mon-Fri 1300-1800, US$1*, preserves intact the household of President Bartolomé Mitre; has a coin and map collection and historical archives.

The **Plaza San Martín** has a monument to San Martín at the western corner of the main park and, at the north end, a memorial with an eternal flame to those who fell in the Falklands/ Malvinas War of 1982. On the plaza is **Palacio San Martín** ① *Arenales 761, T4819 8092, free tours in Spanish and English (check times, tours usually Thu mornings and Fri afternoons)*. Built 1905-1909, it is three houses linked together, now the Foreign Ministry. It has collections of prehispanic and 20th-century art. On the opposite side of the plaza is the opulent **Palacio Paz** (Círculo Militar), ① *Av Santa Fe 750, T4311 1071, www.circulomilitar.org, guided tours Tue-Fri 1100, 1500; Wed and Thu 1600, US$4 (in English Tue and Fri 1530, US$8.25)*. The Círculo Militar includes **Museo de Armas** ① *Av Santa Fe*

Buenos Aires centre

To Palermo Parks & Aeroparque

To Recoleta

Quintana

Guido

Arroyo

Juncal

Arenales

Av del Libertador

11

3

Esmeralda

Basavilbaso

Maipú

Palacio
San Martín

Gral
San Martín

1

5

Av Callao

Montevideo

Pizzurno

Av Santa Fe

32

28

Santa Fe

2

MT de Alvear

3

Plaza
Libertad

2

29

1

12

Paraguay

30

33

39

34

12

41

7

9

Av Córdoba

Cerrito

Pellegrini

Suipacha

11

32

25

25

Callao

Dellepiane

Parana

Uruguay

Talcahuano

Libertad

Plaza
Lavalle

Teatro
Colón

Viamonte

Tucumán

26

12

4

19

31

10

13

18

Tribunales

South American
Explorers

Plaza de la
República &
Obelisk

18

Lavalle

22

13

To La Chacarita
Cemetery

Rodriguez Peña

Montevideo

11

2

Uruguay

4

Av Corrientes

17

13

Carlos
Pellegrini

8

Av Corrientes

37

Callao

13

6

i

9 de Julio

Diagonal
Norte

8

Av Callao

Sarmiento

Juan D Perón

Carabelas

Av R S Peña

Maluca
Beleza

21

Bartolomé Mitre

Congreso

Rivadavia

20

15

Lima

Av de
Mayo

4

Piedras

Plaza del
Congreso

Av de Mayo

3

17

Saenz
Peña

7

Palacio del
Congreso

H Yrigoyen

9

Piedras

Alsina

Lima

Av 9 de Julio

Solís

Virrey Ceballos

E Saenz Peña

San José

Moreno

Santiago del Estero

Salta

Moreno

Belgrano

Tacuari

Roca

Chacabuco

1

To 35 13

2

3

To 35

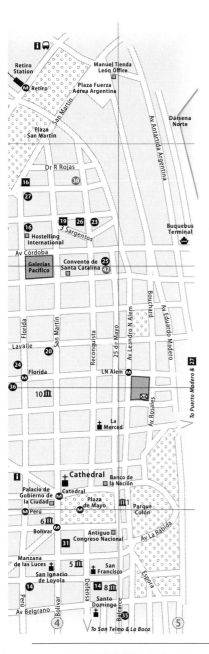

200 metres
200 yards

Sleeping 🛏

06 Central **8** *D3*
Aspen Towers **1** *B3*
BA Stop **34** *D2*
Bisonte Palace **2** *B3*
Castelar **3** *E2*
Clan House **9** *E3*
Lime House **20** *D2*
Colón **4** *C3*
Dolmen **28** *B3*
Dorá **12** *B3*
El Conquistador **29** *B3*
Faena Universe **27** *C5*
Frossard **10** *C4*
Goya **11** *C3*
Hilton **27** *C5*
Hostel Suites
  Obelisco **37** *D3*
Kilca Hostel &
  Backpacker **35** *E1*
La Casa de Etty **13** *E1*
Marbella **15** *E2*
Marriott Plaza **16** *B4*
Milhouse Hostel **17** *E3*
Moreno **14** *E4*
NH City **31** *E4*
O'Rei **18** *C3*
Orly **19** *B4*
Panamericano **12** *C3*
Pestana **30** *B3*
Plaza San Martín
  Suites **32** *B3*
St Nicholas **21** *D1*
V&S **25** *C3*
Waldorf **26** *B4*

Eating 🍴

Abril **1** *B3*
Aroma **27** *B4*
Café de la Biblioteca **3** *B2*
Café Tortoni **4** *D3*
Chiquilín **6** *D1*
Clásica y Moderna **29** *B1*
Confitería Ideal **8** *D3*
Desiderio **5** *B3*
El Gato Negro **11** *C1*
El Palacio de la Papa
  Frita **13** *C3/D1*
El Querandí **14** *E4*

Florida Garden **16** *B4*
Gianni's **25** *B4/C3*
Gran Victoria **32** *C3*
Güerrín **17** *D2*
Il Fratello **31** *C4*
La Casona del
  Nonno **18** *C3*
La Chacra **33** *B3*
La Estancia **19** *C3*
La Pipeta **20** *C4*
La Trastienda **35** *E5*
Los Inmortales **22** *C3*
Morizono **23** *B4*
Palacio Español **7** *E3*
Richmond **24** *C4*
Saint Moritz **39** *B3*
Sattva **2** *C1*
Sorrento **36** *C4*
Tancat **34** *B4*
Tomo 1 **26** *C3*

Bars & clubs 🍸

Druid In **38** *B4*
El Living **41** *B1*
La Cigale **42** *C4*

Museums 🏛

Casa de Gobierno
  (Casa Rosada) &
  Museo de los
  Presidentes **1** *D5*
Museo de Armas **2** *B3*
Museo de Arte
  Hispanoamericano
  Isaac Fernández
  Blanco **3** *A3*
Museo de Arte
  Moderno & Teatro
  General San
  Martín **4** *D1*
Museo de la
  Ciudad **5** *E4*
Museo del Cabildo
  y la Revolución
  de Mayo **6** *E4*
Museo del
  Holocausto **12** *B1*
Museo del Teatro
  Nacional Cervantes **7** *B2*
Museo Etnográfico
  JB Ambrosetti **8** *E4*
Museo Judío **9** *C2*
Museo y Biblioteca
  Mitre **10** *D4*
Museo Nacional
  Ferroviario at Retiro
  Station **11** *A3*

702 y Maipú, Mon-Fri 1300-1900, US$1. It has all kinds of weaponry related to Argentine history, including the 1982 Falklands/ Malvinas War, plus Oriental weapons.

Plaza Fuerza Aérea Argentina (formerly Plaza Británica) has the clock tower presented by British and Anglo-Argentine residents, while in the **Plaza Canadá** (in front of the Retiro Station) there is a Pacific Northwest Indian totem pole, donated by the Canadian government. Behind Retiro station is **Museo Nacional Ferroviario** ① *ring the bell, free, Av del Libertador 405, T4318 3343, Mon-Fri 1000-1600, free.* For railway fans: locomotives, machinery, documents of the Argentine system's history, the building is in very poor condition. In a warehouse beside is the workshop of the sculptor Carlos Regazzoni who recycles refuse material from railways.

Museo de Arte Hispanoamericano Isaac Fernández Blanco ① *Suipacha 1422 (3 blocks west of Retiro), T4326 3396, Tue-Sun, 1400-1900, Thu free, US$0.35, for guided visits in English T4327 0228, tours in Spanish Sat, Sun 1500,* is one of the city's best museums. It contains a fascinating collection of colonial art, especially paintings and silver, also temporary exhibitions of Latin American art, in a beautiful neocolonial mansion (Palacio Noel, 1920s) with Spanish gardens; free concerts and tango lessons on Monday.

Recoleta and Palermo

Nuestra Señora del Pilar, Junín 1898, is a jewel of colonial architecture dating from 1732 (renovated in later centuries), facing onto the public gardens of Recoleta. A fine wooden image of San Pedro de Alcántara, attributed to the famous 17th-century Spanish sculptor Alonso Cano, is preserved in a side chapel on the left, and there are stunning gold altars. Upstairs is an interesting museum of religious art.

Next to it, the **Cemetery of the Recoleta** ① *entrance at Junín 1790, near Museo de Bellas Artes (see below), T4804 7040, 0700-1800, free tours in Spanish Tue-Sun 0900, 1000, 1100, 1400, 1500, 1600 (on Tue and Thu 1100 in English),* is one of the sights of Buenos Aires. With its streets and alleys separating family mausoleums built in every imaginable architectural style, La Recoleta is often compared to a miniature city. Among the famous names from Argentine history is Evita Perón who lies in the Duarte family mausoleum: to find it from the entrance go to the first tree-filled plaza; turn left and where this avenue meets a main avenue (go just beyond the Turriaca tomb), turn right; then take the third passage on the left. On Saturday and Sunday there is a good craft market in the park on Plaza Francia outside the cemetery (1000-2200), with street artists and performers. Next to the cemetery, the **Centro Cultural Recoleta** ① *T4803 1040, www.centroculturalrecoleta.org, Tue-Fri 1400-2100, Sat, Sun, holidays 1000-2100, buses 110, 102, 17, 60 (walk from corner of Las Heras y Junín, 2 blocks) from downtown, eg Correo Central, 61/62, 93, 130 to Av del Libertador y Av Pueyrredón,* specializes in contemporary local art. Next door, the Buenos Aires Design Centre has good design and handicraft shops.

Museo de Bellas Artes (National Gallery) ① *Av del Libertador 1473, T4803 0802, www.mnba.org.ar, Tue-Fri 1230-1930, Sat-Sun 0930-1930, guided tours Tue-Sun 1700, 1800, check tours available for children in summer, free.* This excellent museum gives a taste of Argentine art, as well as a fine collection of European works, particularly post-Impressionist. Superb Argentine 19th and 20th-century paintings, sculpture and wooden carvings; also films, classical music concerts and art courses. **Biblioteca Nacional** (National Library) ① *Av del Libertador 1600 y Agüero 2502, T4808 6000, www.bibnal.edu.ar, Mon-Fri 0900-2000, Sat and Sun 1200-1900, closed Jan.* Housed in a modern building, only a fraction of the extensive stock can be seen. Art gallery, periodical archives; cultural events held. **Museo Nacional de Arte Decorativo** ① *Av del Libertador 1902, T4802 6606, www.mnad.org, Tue-Sun 1400-1900 (Jan-Feb, closed Mon and Sun), US$0.70, guided visits 1630 (at 1430 in English).* It contains collections of painting, furniture, porcelain, crystal, sculpture exhibited in sumptuous halls, once a family residence.

Palermo Chico is a delightful residential area with several houses of once wealthy families, dating from the early 20th-century. The predominant French style of the district was broken in 1929 by the rationalist lines of the **Casa de la Cultura** ① *Rufino de Elizalde 2831, T4808 0553, Tue-Sun 1500-2000 (Jan closed).* The original residence of the writer Victoria Ocampo was a gathering place for artists and intellectuals and is now an attractive cultural centre with art exhibitions and occasional concerts.

Museo de Arte Popular José Hernández ① *Av del Libertador 2373, T4803 2384, www.mujose.org.ar, Wed-Fri 1300-1900, Sat-Sun 1000-2000, US$1, free Sun; for guided tours in English T4803 2384.* The widest collection of Argentine folkloric art, with rooms dedicated to indigenous, colonial and Gaucho artefacts; handicraft shop and library. **Museo de Arte Latinoamericano (MALBA)** ① *Av Figueroa Alcorta 3415, T4808 6500, www.malba.org.ar, daily 1200-1930 (Wed free, open till 2100; Tue closed), US$4 (free for ISIC holders), guided tours in Spanish or English can be booked a week in advance, T4808 6556.* One of the most important museums in the city houses renowned Latin American artists' works: powerful, moving and highly recommended. It's not a vast collection, but representative of the best from the continent. Good library, cinema (showing art house films as well as Argentine classics), seminars and shop, also has an elegant café, serving delicious food and cakes.

Of the fine **Palermo Parks**, the largest is Parque Tres de Febrero, famous for its extensive rose garden, Andalusian Patio, and delightful **Jardín Japonés** (with café) ① *T4804 4922, daily 1000-1800, US$1.70, free guided visits Sat and Sun 1500.* It is a charming place for a walk, delightful for children, and with a good café serving some Japanese dishes. Close by is the **Hipódromo Argentino** (Palermo racecourse) ① *T4778 2800, races 10 days per month, free.* Opposite the parks are the Botanical and Zoological Gardens. At the entrance to the **Planetarium** ① *just off Belisario Roldán, in Palermo Park, T4771 9393, shows at weekends US$1.40; small museum,* are several large meteorites from Campo del Cielo. **Museo de Artes Plásticas Eduardo Sívori** ① *Av Infanta Isabel 555 (Parque Tres de Febrero), T4774 9452, www.museosivori.org.ar, Tue-Fri 1200-2000, Sat and Sun 1000-2000 (1800 in winter), US$0.35 (US$1 for non-residents), Wed free, guided visits Sat and Sun 1600, 1700.* Emphasis on 19th and 20th-century Argentine art, sculpture and tapestry. The **Show Grounds** of the Argentine Rural Society, next to Palermo Park, entrance on Plaza Italia, stage the Annual Livestock Exhibition, known as Exposición Rural, in July. The **Botanical Gardens** ① *Santa Fe 3951, T4831 4527, entrance from Plaza Italia (take Subte, line D) or from C República Arabe Siria, daily 0800-1800, free guided visits Sat-Sun 1030; also nocturnal tours last Fri of each month at 2100 (booking required),* contain characteristic specimens of the world's vegetation. The trees native to the different provinces of Argentina are brought together in one section. One block beyond is **Museo Evita** ① *Lafinur 2988, T4807 9433, Tue-Sun 1300-1900 (Tue-Sun 1100-1900 in summer), US$1 (US$3.40 for non-residents), Tue free for residents; guided visits in Spanish or English on request, only for groups of more than five people.* In a former women's shelter run by Fundación Eva Perón, the exhibition of dresses, paintings and other items is quite interesting though lacks the expected passion; also a library and a café.

There are three important museums in Belgrano: **Museo Histórico Sarmiento** ① *Juramento 2180, T4782 2354, www.museosarmiento.gov.ar, Mon-Fri 1400-1800, Sun 1500-1830 (closed Sun Dec-Mar), US$0.35, Thu free, guided visits on second Sun of the month 1500.* The National Congress and presidential offices in 1880 now houses documents and personal effects of the former president, with a library of his work. **Museo de Arte Español Enrique Larreta** ① *Juramento 2291, T4784 4040, Wed-Fri and Mon, 1500-2000, Sat-Sun 1000-1300, 1500-2000, guided visits Sat-Sun 1600, 1800, US$0.35.* The home of the writer Larreta, with paintings and religious art from the 14th to the 20th century; also has a beautiful garden ① *open Mon-Fri 1000-1300 at Vuelta de Obligado 2155.* **Museo Casa Yrurtia** ① *O'Higgins 2390, esq Blanco Encalada, T/F4781 0385, Tue-Fri 1300-1900, Sun 1500-1900, US$0.35.* An old house crammed with sculpture, paintings, furniture and the collections of artist Rogelio Yrurtia and his wife; peaceful garden.

South of Plaza de Mayo

The church of **San Ignacio de Loyola**, begun 1664, is the oldest colonial building in Buenos Aires (renovated in 18th and 19th centuries). It stands in a block of Jesuit origin, called the **Manzana de las Luces** (Enlightenment Square – Moreno, Alsina, Perú and Bolívar). Also in this block are the **Colegio Nacional de Buenos Aires** ① *Bolívar 263, T4331 0734*, formerly the site of the Jesuits' Colegio Máximo, the Procuraduría de las Misiones (today the Mercado de las Luces, a crafts market) and 18th-century **tunnels** ① *T4342 4655*. For centuries the whole block was the centre of intellectual activity, though little remains today but a small **cultural centre with art courses, concerts, plays and film shows** ① *T4342 4655, www.manzanadelasluces.gov.ar, guided tours from Perú 272, Mon-Fri 1500, Sat and Sun 1500, 1630, 1800 (Mon 1300 free tour) in Spanish (in English by prior arrangement), arrive 15 mins before tour, US$1.70; the tours explore the tunnels and visit the buildings on C Perú, only some weekend tours may include San Ignacio and its cloisters, and Colegio Nacional adding an extra fee.* The **Museo de la Ciudad** ① *Alsina 412, T4343 2123, Mon-Sun 1100-1900, US$0.35 (US$1 for non-residents), free on Wed.* Permanent exhibition covering social history and popular culture, special exhibitions on daily life in Buenos Aires changed every two months, and a reference library open to the public. The church of **San Francisco** ① *Alsina y Defensa, daily 0800-1900*, run by the Franciscan Order, was built 1730-1754 and given a new façade in 1911.

Santo Domingo ① *Defensa y Belgrano, Mon-Fri 0900-1300, Sun 1000-1300*, was founded in 1751. During the British attack on Buenos Aires in 1806 some of Whitelocke's soldiers took refuge in the church. The local forces bombarded it, the British capitulated and their regimental colours were preserved in the church. General Belgrano is buried here. The church holds occasional concerts.

Museo Etnográfico JB Ambrosetti ① *Moreno 350, T4345 8196, www.museo etnografico.filo.uba.ar, Tue-Fri 1300-1900, Sat-Sun 1500-1900 (closed Jan), US$0.70, guided visits Sat-Sun 1600.* Anthropological and ethnographic collections from the Mapuche and Argentina's northwest cultures (the latter a rich collection displayed on the first floor); also a small international room with a magnificent Japanese Buddhist altar.

San Telmo and La Boca

One of the few places which still has late colonial and Rosista buildings (mostly renovated in the 20th century) is the *barrio* of **San Telmo**, south of Plaza de Mayo. It's an atmospheric place, with lots of cafés, antique shops and little art galleries. On Sundays, it has a great atmosphere, with an antiques market at the Plaza Dorrego (see page 88), free tango shows (1000-1800) and live music. The 29 bus connects La Boca with San Telmo.

Parque Lezama, Defensa y Brasil, originally one of the most beautiful in the city, now rather run down and unsafe at night, has an imposing statue of Pedro de Mendoza, who (according to tradition) founded the original city in 1536 on this spot. In the park is the **Museo Histórico Nacional** ① *Defensa 1600, T4307 1182, Tue-Sun 1300-1800, US$0.50, guided tours Sat-Sun 1530.* Argentine history, San Martín's uniforms and the original furniture and door of the house in which he died at Boulogne. In the park is the **Iglesia Ortodoxa Rusa** ① *Brasil 315; visits on Sat afternoon (women wearing trousers will be given skirts; men in shorts will be refused entry),* with its five blue domes and a wonderful interior.

East of the Plaza de Mayo, behind the Casa Rosada, a broad avenue, Paseo Colón, runs south towards San Telmo and as Av Almirante Brown on to the old port district of **La Boca** ① *take bus 152 from Av Santa Fe, or Alem, or bus 29 from Plaza de Mayo, US$0.33,* where the Riachuelo flows into the Plata. The area's distinctive brightly painted tin and wooden houses can be seen along Caminito, the little pedestrian street used as an art market. Visit the **Museo de Bellas Artes Benito Quinquela Martín** ① *Pedro de Mendoza 1835, T4301 1080, Tue-Fri 1000-1730 (in summer opens at 1100), Sat-Sun 1100-1730, closed Jan, US$0.35,* with over 1,000 works by Argentine artists, particularly Benito Quinquela Martín (1890-1977), who painted La Boca port life. Also sculptures and figureheads rescued from ships. La Boca is the poorest and roughest area within central Buenos Aires and tourists are, targets for crime. Don't go alone and stay within the cleaned-up, touristy part of Caminito and along the quay only as far as the museum. Avoid the area at night. The area is especially rowdy when the Boca Juniors football club is playing at home. At Boca Juniors stadium is **Museo de la Pasión Boquense** ① *Brandsen 805, T4362 1100, www.museoboquense.com, daily 1000-1800 (opening times may change during matches), US$4.70 for non-residents. Guided tour of the stadium in Spanish or English, 1100-1700, plus ticket to the museum, US$7 for non-residents.*

Docks and Costanera Sur
Fragata Presidente Sarmiento ① *dock 3, Av Dávila y Perón, Puerto Madero, T4334 9386, daily 1030-1930 (closed on rainy days), US$0.70.* A naval training ship until 1961; now a museum. Nearby, in dock 4, is the **Corbeta Uruguay** ① *T4314 1090, daily 1400-1800 (closed on rainy days), 1100-1900 in summer, free,* the ship that rescued Otto Nordenskjold's Antarctic expedition in 1903. The **Puerto Madero** dock area has been renovated; the 19th-century warehouses are restaurants and bars, an attractive place for a stroll and popular nightspot. East of San Telmo on the far side of the docks, the Avenida Costanera runs as a long, spacious boulevard. A stretch of marshland reclaimed from the river forms the interesting **Costanera Sur Wildlife Reserve** ① *entrances at Av Tristán Achával Rodríguez 1550 (take Estados Unidos east from San Telmo) or next to the Buquebús ferry terminal (take Av Córdoba east), T4315 4129; for pedestrians and bikers only, Tue-Sun 0800-1800 (in summer, closes at 1900), free, bus 2 passes next to the southern entrance,* where there are over 200 species of birds, including the curve-billed reed hunter. Free guided tours at weekends 1030, 1530, from the administration next to the southern entrance, but much can be seen from the road before then (binoculars useful). Also free nocturnal visits every month on the Friday closest to the full moon and the following Thursday (book Monday before, reserva_cs@buenos

aires.gov.ar). It's half an hour walk from the entrance to the river shore and about three hours to walk the whole perimeter. In summer it's very hot with little shade. For details (particularly birdwatching) contact Aves Argentinas/AOP (see page).

Around Buenos Aires

Tigre → *Population: 31,000 (Partido de Tigre –Tigre county – 301,000).*
This touristy little town, 32 km northwest of Buenos Aires, is a popular weekend destination lying on the lush jungly banks of the Río Luján, with a fun fair and an excellent fruit and handicrafts market (Puerto de Frutos) daily 1000-1900 with access from Calles Sarmiento or Perú. There are restaurants on the waterfront in Tigre across the Río Tigre from the railway line, along Lavalle and Paseo Victorica (eg **María del Luján** is recommended); cheaper places can be found on Italia and Cazón on the near side, or at the Puerto de Frutos. North of the town is the delta of the Río Paraná: innumerable canals and rivulets, with holiday homes and restaurants on the banks and a fruit-growing centre. The fishing is excellent and the peace is only disturbed by motor-boats at weekends. Regattas are held in November. Take a trip on one of the regular launch services (*lanchas colectivas*) which run to all parts of the delta, including taxi launches – watch prices for these – from the wharf (*Estación Fluvial*). Tourist catamarans, five services daily, 1-2 hour trips, US$7-10, from Lavalle 499 on Río Tigre, T4731 0261/63, www.tigreencatamaran. com.ar, and three to eight services daily, 1½-hour trips, US$8, from Puerto de Frutos, *Río Tur* (T4731 0280, www.rioturcatamaranes.com.ar). *Sturla* (Estación Fluvial, oficina 10, T4731 1300, www.sturla viajes.com.ar) runs three 1-hour trips a day, US$6, to which can be added a lunch at Villa Julia, exclusive restaurante in Tigre (US$26) or a barbecue at an island with a daily half-day tour (US$21); also full-day tours that include lunch and kayak excursions for US$31 and 1½-hour trips to Puerto Norte (next to Aeroparque) on the Río de la Plata for US$15 pp. **Tigre tourist office** ① *Lavalle y R Fernández, T4512 4497, 0900-1700, www.tigre.gov.ar.* **Centro de Guías de Tigre y Delta** ① *Estación Fluvial oficina 2, T4731 3555, www.tododelta.com.ar.* For guided walks and launch trips.

Museo Naval ① *Paseo Victorica 602, T4749 0608, Mon-Fri 0830-1730, Sat-Sun 1030-1830, US$1.* Worth a visit to see the displays on the Argentine navy. There are also relics of the 1982 Falklands/ Malvinas War. **Museo de Arte** ① *Paseo Victoria 972, T4512 4528, Wed-Fri 0900-1900, Sat-Sun 1200-1900 (closes at 1800 in winter), US$1.70,* hosts a collection of Argentine figurative art in the former Tigre Club Casino, a beautiful belle époque building. **Museo del Mate** ① *Lavalle 289, T4506 9594, www.elmuseodelmate.com, Tue-Sun 1000-1800, US$2.60,* tells the history of mate and has an interesting collection of the associated paraphernalia.

Isla Martín García

This island in the Río de la Plata (Juan Díaz de Solís' landfall in 1516) used to be a military base. Now it is an ecological/historical centre and an ideal excursion from the capital, with many trails through the cane brakes, trees and rocky outcrops – interesting birds and flowers. Boat trips: four weekly from Tigre at 0900, returning 2000, three-hour journey, US$17 return (US$32 including lunch and guide; US$73 including weekend overnight at inn, full board). Reservations only through *Cacciola* (address under Tigre, Transport, below), who also handle bookings for the inn and restaurant on the island. There is also a campsite.

Buenos Aires listings

For Sleeping and Eating price codes and other relevant information, see pages 8-9.

😴 Sleeping

Hotels in the upper ranges can often be booked more cheaply through Buenos Aires travel agencies. The tourist offices at Ezeiza and Jorge Newbery airports book rooms. If you pay in pesos in cash you may get a reduction. Room tax (VAT) is 21% and is not always included in the price. A/c is a must in high summer. Finding hotels for Fri, Sat, Sun nights can be difficult and hostels can get very busy, resulting in pressure on staff. The range of `boutique' hotels and hostels is impressive, especially in Palermo and San Telmo. The same applies to restaurants, bars and clubs. There are far more than we can list here, but between this book and Footprint's *Argentina Handbook*, we hope to have covered a good selection. There are fine examples of the **Four Seasons** (www.fourseasons.com/ buenosaires), **N/A Town & Country Hotels** (www.newage-hotels.com), **Hilton** (www.hilton.com), **Marriott** (www.marriott.com) **NH** (www.nh-hoteles.com), **Pestana** (www.pestana.com), **Sofitel** (www.sofitel.com) and **Unique Hotels** (www.hotels-unique.com) chains. Hotels will store luggage, and most have English-speaking staff.

Centre *p66, map p68*

$$$$ Alvear Palace, Av Alvear 1891, T4808 2100, reservations 4804 7777, www.alvear palace.com. The height of elegance, an impeccably preserved 1920s Recoleta palace, sumptuous marble foyer, with Louis XV-style chairs, and a charming orangery where you can take tea with superb patisseries. Antique-filled bedrooms. Recommended.
$$$$ Art, Azcuénaga 1268, T4821 6248, www.art hotel.com.ar. Charming boutique hotel on a quiet residential street, only a few blocks from Recoleta or Av Santa Fe, simply but warmly decorated, good service, solarium, compact standard rooms.
$$$$ Aspen Towers, Paraguay 857, T5166 1900, www.aspentowers.com.ar. A modern minimalist foyer in this small hotel belies the traditional 1900 French-style bedrooms, all with jacuzzi baths, and all facilities, including a good breakfast and a pool.
$$$$ Bisonte Palace, MT de Alvear 910, T4328 4751, www.hotelesbisonte.com. Charming, with calm entrance foyer, which remains gracious thanks to courteous staff. Plain but spacious rooms, ample breakfast, good location. Very good value.
$$$$ Colón, Carlos Pellegrini 507, T4320 3500, www.colon-hotel.com.ar. Splendid location overlooking Av 9 de Julio and Teatro Colón, extremely good value. Charming bedrooms, comfortable, pool, gym, great breakfasts, and perfect service. Highly recommended.
$$$$ El Conquistador, Suipacha 948, T4328 3012, www.elconquistador.com.ar. Stylish '70s boutique hotel, which retains the wood and chrome foyer, but has bright modern rooms, and a lovely light restaurant on the 10th floor with great views. Well situated, good value.
$$$$ Etoile, R Ortiz 1835 in Recoleta, T4805 2626, www.etoile.com.ar. Outstanding location, rooftop pool, rooms with kitchenette.
$$$$ Faena Universe, Martha Salotti 445 (Puerto Madero), T4010 9000, www.faena hoteland universe.com. Set in a 100-year-old silo, renovated by Philippe Starck, this is not for all budgets or tastes. Eclectic decoration, staff trained to be perfect, the whole place is unique.
$$$$ Panamericano, Carlos Pellegrini 551, T4348 5000, www.panamericano.us. Very smart and modern hotel, with luxurious and tasteful rooms, covered rooftop pool,

and superb restaurant, Tomo 1. Excellent service too.

$$$$ Plaza San Martín Suites, Suipacha 1092, T5093 7000, www.plazasanmartin. com.ar. Neat modern self-contained apartments right in the city centre, comfortable and attractively decorated, with lounge and little kitchen. Sauna, gym, room service. Good value.

$$$ Castelar, Av de Mayo 1152, T4383 5000, www.castelarhotel.com.ar. A wonderfully elegant 1920s hotel which retains all the original features in the grand entrance and bar. Cosy bedrooms, charming staff, and excellent value. Also a spa with turkish baths and massage. Highly recommended.

$$$ Dolmen, Suipacha 1079, T4315 7117, www.hoteldolmen.com.ar. Good location, smart spacious entrance lobby, with a calm relaxing atmosphere, good professional service, modern, comfortable well-designed rooms, small pool.

$$$ Dorá, Maipú 963, T4312 7391, www.dora hotel.com.ar. Charming and old-fashioned with comfortable rooms, good service, attractive lounge with paintings. Warmly recommended.

$$$ Moreno, Moreno 376, T6091 2000, www.morenobuenosaires.com. 150 m to Plaza de Mayo, decorated in dark, rich tones, large rooms, good value, jacuzzi, gym and chic bar. Recommended.

$$$ Orly, Paraguay 474, T/F4312 5344, www.orly.com.ar. Good location, and comfortable plain rooms, with helpful service.

$$$ Waldorf, Paraguay 450, T4312 2071, www.waldorf-hotel.com.ar. Welcoming staff and a comfortable mixture of traditional and modern in this centrally located hotel. Good value, with a buffet breakfast, English spoken. Recommended.

$$ The Clan House, Alsina 817, T4331 4448, www.bedandbreakfastclan.com.ar. Brightly-coloured, modern rooms, buffet breakfast, Wi-Fi and a small terrace, very good.

$$ Frossard, Tucumán 686, T4322 1811, www.hotelfrossard.com.ar. A lovely old 1940s building with high ceilings and the original doors, attractively modernized, and though the rooms are small (avoid No 11), the staff are welcoming, and this is good value, near C Florida.

$$ Goya, Suipacha 748, T4322 9269, www.goya hotel.com.ar. Welcoming and central, worth paying more for superior rooms, though all are comfortable. Good breakfast, English spoken.

$$ Marbella, Av de Mayo 1261, T4383 3573, www.hotelmarbella.com.ar. Modernized and central, though quiet, breakfast included, multi-lingual. Recommended.

$ O'Rei, Lavalle 733, T4393 7186, www.hotel orei.com.ar. Cheaper without bath, central, simple but comfortable, spotless, laundry facilities, helpful staff, no breakfast.

Youth hostels

$ pp 06 Central, Maipú 306, T5219 0052, www.06centralhostel.com. A few metres from the Obelisco and Av Corrientes, simple, spacious dorms, nicely decorated doubles (**$$**), use of kitchen, cosy communal area.

$ pp BA Stop, Rivadavia 1194, T4382 7406, www.bastop.com. Dorms, private rooms (**$$** double), breakfast included, large-screen TV, pool tables, bar, internet, English spoken, safe, very helpful staff. Repeatedly recommended.

$ pp Hostel Suites Obelisco, Av Corrientes 830, T4328 4040, www.hostelsuites.com. Elegant hostel built in a completely restored old building in the heart of the city. Dorms, **$$** doubles and private apartments, breakfast included, DVD room, free internet and Wi-Fi, laundry service. HI discount.

$ pp Limehouse, Lima 11, T4383 4561, www.limehouse.com.ar. Dorms for up to 12 and doubles with and without bath (**$**), popular, typical city hostel with kitchen, internet, bar, roof terrace, "chilled", great if you like the party atmosphere, efficient staff. Recommended.

$ pp Milhouse Hostel, Hipólito Yrigoyen 959, T4383 9383, www.milhousehostel.com. In 1890 house, lovely rooms (**$$**) in double) and dorms, comfortable, free breakfast, cooking facilities, laundry, internet, tango lessons, HI discounts, very popular so reconfirm bookings at all times.

$ pp St Nicholas, B Mitre 1691 (y Rodríguez Peña), T4373 5920/8841, www.snhostel.com. Beautifully converted old house, now a party hostel with spotless rooms but beds could be better, cooking facilities, large roof terrace and a pub with daily live shows, luggage store; also **$ double rooms. Discounts for HI members.

$ pp V&S, Viamonte 887, T4322 0994, www.hostelclub.com. Central popular hostel (**$$** in attractive double room, bath), breakfast, café, tiny kitchen, internet, lockers, tango classes, tours, warm atmosphere, welcoming. Recommended.

Palermo *p70*

$$$$ Bo Bo, Guatemala 4882, T4774 0505, www.bobohotel.com. On a leafy street, 7 rooms decorated in contemporary style, some with private balconies, excellent restaurant.

$$$$ La Otra Orilla, Julián Alvarez 1779, Palermo Viejo, T4863 7426, www.otraorilla. com.ar. Homely, quiet, French-style 1930s residence with 7 very different rooms, from a great suite to a cute single. Some have a balcony or street views, others are more secluded. The patio is delightful for having breakfast in summer. Very good value.

$$$$ Malabia House, Malabia 1555, Palermo Viejo, T4833 2410, www.malabia house.com.ar. Elegant but expensive B&B with individually designed bedrooms and calm sitting rooms, great breakfast, reliable and welcoming. Recommended.

$$$ Krista, Bonpland 1665, T4771 4697, www.kristahotel.com.ar. Intimate, hidden behind the plain façade of an elegant townhouse, well-placed for restaurants. Good

value, comfortable, individually-designed spacious rooms, Wi-Fi, wheelchair access.

$$$ Bernarda House, Uriarte 1942, T4774 8997, www.bernardahouse.com.ar. Quiet, tastefully decorated family home for a relaxing stay, owned and run by welcoming Bernarda and Carlos. Pool, excellent food on request.

$$$ Solar Soler, Soler 5676, T4776 3065, www.solarsoler.com.ar. Homely, welcoming B&B in Palermo Hollywood, excellent service, free internet. Recommended.

$$ Che Lulu, Emilio Zola 5185, T4772 0289, www.chelulu.com. Double rooms and hostel-style accommodation (**$ pp) in this rambling, laid-back house on a quiet quaint street a few blocks from Palermo subte. Not luxurious, but great value and very welcoming. Often recommended.

Youth hostels

$ pp Casa Esmeralda, Honduras 5765, T4772 2446, www.casaesmeralda.com.ar. Laid-back, dorms and **$** doubles, neat garden with hammocks and pond. Sebastián offers basic comfort with great charm.

$ pp Hostel Suites Palermo, Charcas 4752, T4773 0806, www.suitespalermo.com. A beautiful century-old residence with the original grandeur partially preserved and a quiet atmosphere. Comfortable renovated dorms and private rooms with bath (**$$** doubles), good service, small travel agency, free internet, Wi-Fi, cooking and laundry facilities, DVD room and breakfast included.

$ pp Hostal El Candil, Lerma 476, T4899 1547, www.hostalelcandil.com. Argentine-Italian owned hostel with shared rooms and doubles (**$ pp), international atmosphere, quiet, comfortable, welcoming, with breakfast, rooftop terrace, Wi-Fi, tours arranged.

$ pp Tango Backpackers Hostel, Paraguay 4601, T4776 6871, www.tangobp.com. Well situated for Palermo's nightlife, lots of activities, free internet access and Wi-Fi, open terrace with outdoor showers. HI discount.

San Telmo and around *p72*

$$$$ Axel Hotel, Venezuela 649, T4136 9393, ww.axelhotels.com. Stunning gay hotel with 5 floors of stylishly designed rooms, each floor with a cosy living area, rooftop pool, gourmet restaurant. Recommended.

$$$$ Mansión Dandi Royal, Piedras 922, T4307 7623, www.hotelmansiondandi royal.com. A wonderfully restored 1903 residence, small upmarket hotel with an elegant tango atmosphere, small pool, good value. Daily tango lessons and *milonga* every Wed.

$$$ The Cocker, Av Garay 458, T4362 8451, ww.thecocker.com. In the heart of the antiques district, tastefully restored art nouveau house, stylish suites, living room, roof terraces and gardens. Recommended.

$$$ La Casita de San Telmo, Cochabamba 286, T4307 5073, www.lacasitadesantelmo. com. 7 rooms in restored 1840's house, most open onto a garden with a beautiful fig tree, owners are tango fans; rooms rented by day, week or month.

$$ The Four, Carlos Calvo 535, T4362 1729, www.thefourhotel.com. 1930s building converted into a lovely B & B with 6 rooms, appealing terrace, welcoming staff. Recommended.

$$ Garden House Art Factory, Piedras 545, T4343 1463, www.artfactoryba.com.ar. Large, early 1900s house converted into a hotel, charming owners (see **Garden House**, below), informal atmosphere with individually designed and brightly painted private rooms (some with bath), halfway between the centre and San Telmo. Wi-Fi, free internet, breakfast included.

$$ Lugar Gay de Buenos Aires, Defensa 1120 (no sign), T4300 4747, www.lugargay. com.ar. A men-only gay B & B with 8 comfortable rooms, video room, jacuzzi, a stone's throw from Plaza Dorrego.

Youth hostels

$$ Ostinatto, Chile 680, T4362 9639, www.ostinatto.com. Double rooms with and without bath, shared rooms **$** pp, also has an apartment for rent. Minimalist contemporary design in a 1920s building, very nice, communal kitchen, free internet, Wi-Fi, promotes the arts, music, piano bar, movie room, tango lessons, arranges events, rooftop terrace.

$ pp Che Lagarto, Venezuela 857, T4343 4845, www.chelagarto.com. Between Monserrat and San Telmo, large light dorms and **$$** doubles with private bath, TV and fan. Attractive tango hall, the ground floor is a pub and restaurant. Price includes breakfast and free internet.

$ pp El Hostal de Granados, Chile 374, T43625600, www.hostaldegranados.com.ar. Small, light, well-equipped rooms in an interesting building on a popular street, rooms for 2 (**$$**) to 4, with bath, breakfast included, kitchen, free internet and Wi-Fi, laundry.

$ pp Garden House, Av San Juan 1271, T4304 1824, www.gardenhouseba.com.ar. Small, welcoming independent hostel for those who don't want a party atmosphere; good barbecues on the terrace. Includes breakfast, free internet, some more expensive doubles. Recommended.

$ pp Hostel-Inn Buenos Aires, Humberto Primo 820, T4300 7992, www.hibuenosaires. com. An old 2-storey mansion with an outdoor terrace, dorms for up to 8 people and also private rooms, activities, loud parties, free internet and Wi-Fi, breakfast included and individual lockers in every room. HI discount.

$ pp Hostel-Inn Tango City, Piedras 680, T4300 5776, www.hitangocity.com. Well organized in renovated house with varied dorms and private rooms, popular, lively, parties, lots of activities, breakfast, DVD room, free internet access and Wi-Fi. HI discount.

$ pp Kilca Hostel & Backpacker, Mexico 1545, between Saenz Peña and Virrey Cevallos, T4381 1966, www.kilcabackpacker. com. Lovingly restored 19th-century house with attractive landscaped patios. A variety of rooms from dorms to doubles; all bathrooms shared. Wi-Fi, breakfast included.

$ pp Sandanzas, Balcarce 1351, T4300 7375, www.sandanzas.com.ar. Arty hostel run by a group of friends. Small but with a light airy feel, more expensive doubles with bath, lounge and patio, free internet, Wi-Fi, breakfast and use of bikes, DVDs, kitchen.

Homestays and student residences

B&T Argentina, T4876 5000, www.byt argentina.com. Accommodation in student residences and host families; also furnished flats.

La Casa de Etty, Luis Sáenz Peña 617, T4384 6378, info@coret.com.ar. Run by Esther Corcias, manager of **Organización Coret**, www.angelfire. com/pq/coret. Host families.

Apartments/self catering

Bahouse, T4815 7602, www.bahouse.com.ar. Very good flats, by the week or month (from US$170 per week), all furnished and well-located in San Telmo, Retiro, Recoleta, Belgrano, Palermo and the centre.

Tu Casa Argentina, Esmeralda 980, p 2B, T4312 4127, www.tucasargentina.com. Furnished flats by the day, week, month (from US$40 per day). Credit cards not accepted, deposit and rent payable in dollars. Efficient and helpful.

❼ Eating

Eating out in Buenos Aires is one of the city's great pleasures, with a huge variety of restaurants from the chic to the cheap. To try some of Argentina's excellent steak, choose from one of the many *parrillas*, where your huge slab of lean meat will be expertly cooked over a wood fire. If in doubt about where to eat, head for Puerto Madero, where

there are lots of good places serving international as well as local cuisine. Take a taxi to Palermo or Las Cañitas for a wide range of excellent restaurants all within strolling distance. For more information on the gastronomy of Buenos Aires see: www.guiaoleo.com.ar, restaurant guide in Spanish and English; www.vidalbuzzi.com.ar, in Spanish. 2 fantastic food-oriented blogs in English are: www.saltshaker.net, chef Dan Pearlman who also runs a highly recommended private restaurant in his house, see website for details; and www.foodquests.blogspot.com, international food writer Layne Molser. Some restaurants are *tenedor libre*: eat as much as you like for a fixed price. Most cafés serve tea or coffee plus *facturas*, or pastries, for breakfast, US$1.50-3.

Retiro, and the area between Plaza de Mayo and Plaza San Martín *p66, map p68*

$$$ Chiquilín, Sarmiento 1599. *Parrilla* and pasta. Good atmosphere, though a little overpriced.

$$$ El Querandí, Perú 302 y Moreno. Good food in an intimate atmosphere in this place that was opened in the 1920s and is now also a tango venue in the evening. Next door is a wine bar serving lunch and dinner at **La Cava del Querandí**, Perú 322.

$$$ La Chacra, Av Córdoba 941 (just off 9 de Julio). A superb traditional *parrilla* with excellent steaks (US$24 for parrillada for 2), impeccable old-fashioned service, lively atmosphere.

$$$ Morizono, Reconquista 899. Japanese dishes. Recommended for their set lunch menus.

$$$ Palacio Español at the Club Español, B de Irigoyen 180 (on Av 9 de Julio, near Av de Mayo). Originally a sumptuous room in a fine building, recommended for a quiet dinner, with excellent food, basically Spanish dishes.

$$$ Sorrento Corrientes 668 (just off Florida). Intimate, elegant atmosphere, one of the most traditional places in the centre for very good pastas and seafood.

$$$ Tancat, Paraguay 645. Delicious Spanish food, very popular at lunchtime.

$$$ Tomo 1, Panamericano Hotel, Carlos Pellegrini 521, T4326 6695. Argentine regional dishes and international cuisine of a high standard in a sophisticated atmosphere. Very expensive.

$$ Abril, Suipacha y Arenales. A good small place serving a varied menu.

$$ El Palacio de la Papa Frita, Lavalle 735 and 954, Corrientes 1620. Great place for a filling feed, with a large menu, and quite atmospheric, despite the bright lighting.

$$ Gianni´s, Viamonte 834 and Reconquista 1028. The set menu with the meal-of-the-day makes an ideal lunch. Good risottos and salads.

$$ Güerrín, Corrientes 1368. A Buenos Aires institution. Serves filling pizza and *faina* (chick pea polenta) which you eat standing up at a bar, or at tables, though you miss out on the colourful local life that way. Wonderful. For an extra service fee, upstairs room is less crowded or noisy.

$$ Il Fratello, Tucumán 688. Popular for pasta at lunchtime.

$$ La Casona del Nonno, Lavalle 827. Popular with tourists, for its central location and for its set price menu serving good food.

$$ La Estancia, Lavalle 941. A slightly touristy but reliable *parrilla*, popular with business people at lunchtime, good grills, *parrillada* US$20 for 2.

$$ La Pipeta, San Martín 498. A traditional, unpretentious place, established 40 years, for good food in a noisy atmosphere, closed Sun.

$$ Los Inmortales, Lavalle 746. Specializes in pizza, tasty, good value, great salads, good service.

$$ Sattva, Montevideo 446. A healthy and relaxing oasis next to the busy pizzerías district on Av Corrientes, serving vegetarian and vegan dishes. The meal of the day for lunch is always a good choice. Closed on Sun.

R **Gran Victoria**, Suipacha 783. Good value *tenedor libre*, including parrilla, in a cheery atmosphere, also cheap set meals.

Cafés

Aroma, Florida y M T de Alvear. A great place to relax, with a huge space upstairs, comfortable chairs for watching the world go by.

Café de la Biblioteca, M T de Alvear 1155 (Asociación Biblioteca de Mujeres). Coffee and light snacks, evening shows.

Café Tortoni, Av de Mayo 825-9. This most famous Buenos Aires café has been the elegant haunt of artists and writers for over 100 years, with marble columns, stained glass ceilings, old leather chairs, and photographs of its famous clientele on the walls. Excellent coffee and cakes, good tea, excellent tango, live jazz in evenings, all rather pricey. Getting increasingly packed with tourists, but still worth a visit.

Clásica y Moderna, Callao 892, T4812 8707, www.clasicaymoderna.com. One of the city's most welcoming cafés, with a bookshop, great atmosphere, good breakfast through to drinks at night, daily live music and varied shows. Highly recommended.

Confitería Ideal, Suipacha 384. One of the most atmospheric cafés in the city. Wonderfully old-fashioned 1930s interior, serving good coffee and excellent cakes with good service. Upstairs, tango is taught and there's tango dancing at a *milonga* here. Highly recommended.

Desiderio, Av Santa Fe y Esmeralda. Good coffee and drinks, in a nice, though noisy corner on plaza San Martín.

El Gato Negro, Av Corrientes 1669. A beautiful tearoom, serving a choice of coffees and teas, and good cakes. Delightfully scented from the wide range of spices on sale.

Florida Garden, Florida y Paraguay. Another well-known café, popular for lunch, and tea.
Richmond, Florida 468, between Lavalle and Corrientes. Genteel, old fashioned and charming place for tea with cakes, and a basement where chess is played between 1200-2400 daily.
Saint Moritz, Esmeralda y Paraguay. Original late 1950s decor with a particularly calm atmosphere on a very busy corner.

The Italian ice cream tradition has been marked for decades by 'heladerías' such as **Cadore**, Av Corrientes 1695 or **El Vesuvio**, Av Corrientes 1181, the oldest of all.

West of Plaza de Mayo *p66*
3 blocks west of Plaza San Martín, under the flyover at the northern end of Av 9 de Julio, between Arroyo and Av del Libertador in La Recova, are several recommended restaurants.
$$$ El Mirasol de la Recova, Posadas 1032. Serves top-quality parrilla in an elegant atmosphere.
$$$ La Tasca de Plaza Mayor, Posadas 1052. Very good Spanish tapas and attentive service.
$$$ Piegari, Posadas 1042. Great for Italian food served in generous portions; though a bit overpriced and a noisy place.
$$ Juana M, Carlos Pellegrini 1535 (downstairs). Excellent choice, popular with locals for its good range of dishes, and its very good salad bar.
$$ Winery, Paseo La Recova, off Libertador 500. A chic wine bar where you can sample the best of Argentina's fine wines, light dishes such as salads and gourmet sandwiches. Also at Av Alem 880 and Juana Manso 835 (Puerto Madero).

Recoleta *p70*
$$$ Lola, Roberto M Ortiz 1805. Well known for superb pasta dishes, lamb and fish.
$$$ Sirop, Pasaje del Correo, Vte Lopez 1661, T4813 5900. Delightful chic design, delicious

French-inspired food, superb patisserie too. Highly recommended.
$$ El Sanjuanino, Posadas 1515. Atmospheric place offering typical dishes from the northwest: *humitas*, *tamales*, and *empanadas*, as well as unusual game dishes.
$$ La Madeleine, Av Santa Fe 1726. Open 24 hrs. Bright and cheerful choices; quite good pastas.
$$ María de Bambi, Ayacucho 1821. This small, quiet place is probably the best value in the area, serving very good and simple meals. Open till 2130, closed on Sun.
$$ Rodi Bar, Vicente López 1900. Excellent *bife* and other dishes in this typical *bodegón*, welcoming and unpretentious.

Tea rooms, café-bars and ice cream
Café Victoria, Roberto M Ortiz 1865. Wonderful old-fashioned café, popular and refined, great cakes.
Ice Cream Freddo, in Recoleta at Roberto M Ortiz y Quintana, Arenales y Callao, Roberto M Ortiz y Guido, Santa Fe y Montevideo and at shopping malls. Known for the best ice cream.
Milion, Paraná 1048. Stylish bar and café in an elegant mansion with marble stairs and a garden, young and cool clientèle.
Un'Altra Volta, in Recoleta at Av Santa Fe y Av Callao, Quintana y Ayacucho, Pacheco de Melo y Av Callao. Great ice creams.

Palermo *p70*
This area of Buenos Aires is very popular, with many chic restaurants and bars in Palermo Viejo (referred to as 'Palermo Soho' for the area next to Plaza Cortázar and 'Palermo Hollywood' for the area beyond the railways and Av Juan B Justo) and the Las Cañitas district. It's a sprawling district, so you could take a taxi to one of these restaurants, and walk around before deciding where to eat. It's also a great place to stop for lunch, with cobbled streets, and 1900s buildings, now housing chic clothes shops.

The Las Cañitas area is fashionable, with a wide range of interesting restaurants mostly along CBaez, and most opening at around 2000, though only open for lunch at weekends:

$$$ Baez, Baez 240, Las Cañitas. Very trendy, with lots of orange neon, serving sophisticated Italian-style food and sushi.

$$$ Cluny, El Salvador 4618, T4831 7176. Very classy, a great place for lunch, fish and pasta with great sauces, mellow music.

$$$ Dominga, Honduras 5618, T4771 4443, www.domingarestaurant.com. Elegant, excellent food from a short but creative menu, professional service, good wine list, ideal for a romantic meal or treat, open evenings only.

$$$ Eh! Santino, Baez 194, Las Cañitas. Italian-style food in a trendy, small, if not cramped place, dark and cosy with lots of mirrors.

$$$ El Manto, Costa Rica 5801, T4774 2409. Genuine Armenian dishes, relaxed, good for a quiet evening.

$$$ Janio, Malabia 1805, T4833 6540. One of Palermo's first restaurants, open for breakfast through to the early hours, lunch US$6, sophisticated Argentine cuisine in the evening.

$$$ Novecento, Baez 199, Las Cañitas. A lively French-style bistro, stylish but unpretentious and cosy, good fish dishes among a broad menu.

$$ Bio, Humboldt 2199, T4774 3880. Delicious gourmet organic food, on a sunny corner, open daily, but closed Mon for dinner.

$$ Campo Bravo, Baez y Arevalo, Las Cañitas. Stylish, minimalist, superb steaks and vegetables on the *parrilla*. Popular and recommended, can be noisy.

$$ De la Ostia, Baez 212, Las Cañitas. A small, chic bistro for tapas and Spanish-style food, good atmosphere.

$$ El Preferido de Palermo, Borges y Guatemala, T4778 7101. Very popular *bodegón* serving both Argentine and Spanish-style dishes.

$$ Eterna Cadencia, Honduras 5574, T4774 4100. A small bookshop with a café which is perfect for lunch, open 0900-2000.

$$ Krishna, Malabia 1833. A small, intimate place serving very good Indian-flavoured vegetarian dishes.

$$ La Cupertina, Cabrera y Godoy Cruz. The attention may be a bit brusque sometimes, but the northwestern Argentine dishes, plus the filling desserts are not to be missed, especially on a cold winter's day.

$$ Morelia, Baez 260, Las Cañitas. Cooks superb pizzas on the *parrilla* or in wood ovens, and has a lovely roof terrace for summer. Also at Humboldt 2005.

$$ Omm, Honduras 5656, T4774 4224. Cosy wine and tapas bar with good food. Also **Omm Carnes**, Costa Rica 5198, T4773 0954, for meat dishes and steak, open from 1800, closed Sun.

$$ Social Paraíso, Honduras 5182. Simple delicious dishes in a relaxed chic atmosphere, with a lovely patio at the back. Good fish and tasty salads. Closed Sun evening and Mon.

$ Palermo DC, Guatemala y Carranza. Surely there is a great chef behind the excellent light meals, sandwiches, salads and vegetable pies served at just few unpretentious tables on the pavement.

Tea rooms, café-bars and ice cream

Palermo has good cafés opposite the park on Av del Libertador, including the fabulous ice creams at **Un'Altra Volta**, Av del Libertador 3060 (another branch at Echeverría 2302, Belgrano).

Persicco, Salguero y Cabello, Maure y Migueletes and Av Rivadavia 4933 (Caballito). The grandsons of **Freddo**'s founders also offer excellent ice cream.

Cheap eats

A few supermarkets have good, cheap restaurants: **Coto** supermarket, Viamonte y Paraná, upstairs. Many supermarkets have very good deli counters and other shops sell *fiambres* (smoked, cured meats) and cheeses for quick, cheap eating. The snack bars in underground stations are also cheap.

Delicity bakeries, several branches, have very fresh *facturas* (pastries), cakes, breads, and American doughnuts. Another good bakery for breakfasts, sandwishes and salads is **Bonpler**, Florida 481, 0730-2300, with the daily papers, classical music. Other branches elsewhere.

San Telmo p72

$$$ La Brigada, Estados Unidos 461, T4361 5557. Atmospheric *parrilla*, serving excellent Argentine cuisine and wines. Very popular and compact, expensive, but recommended. Always reserve.

$$ Brasserie Petanque, Defensa y Mexico. Very attractive, informal French restaurant offering a varied menu with very good, creative dishes. Excellent value for their set lunch menus. Expect slow service.

$$ El Desnivel, Defensa 855. Popular parrilla, packed at weekends, good atmosphere.

$$ Lezama, Brasil 359 (on Parque Lezama). Typical *bodegón*, popular with families, typical Argentine menu, huge portions, rather slow service.

$$ Maraxe, Tacuarí y Chile. A reliable traditional Spanish-style place with good service, with seafood as its speciality.

$ La Trastienda, Balcarce 460. Theatre café with lots of live events, also serving meals and drinks from breakfast to dinner, great music, relaxed and cool, but busy lunchtime. Recommended.

$ Mi Tío, Defensa 900. A small basic place suitable for pizzas and *milanesas*, beloved by San Telmo locals.

Ice creams

Dylan, Perú 1086. Very good. **Freddo**, a few blocks away, at Defensa y Estados Unidos, has opened a new branch.

Puerto Madero p73

The revamped docks area is an attractive place to eat, and to stroll along the waterfront before dinner. There are good places here, generally in stylish interiors and with good service if a little overpriced: along Av Alicia Moreau de Justo (from north to south), these are recommended.

$$$ Cabaña Las Lilas, No 516. Excellent *parrilla*, popular with tourists.

$$$ El Mirasol, No 202. Very good parrilla.

$$$ Katrine, No 138. Smart, with delicious fish and pasta.

$$$ La Parolaccia, Nos 1052 and 1170. Excellent pasta and Italian-style dishes (seafood is the speciality at No 1170), executive lunch US$8 Mon-Fri, popular.

$$$-$$ Fresh Market, Azucena Villaflor y Olga Cossettini. Fresh fruits and vegetables served in the most varied ways in this small, trendy restaurant and deli, from breakfasts to dinners.

Bars and clubs

Generally it is not worth going to clubs before 0230 at weekends. Dress is usually smart.

Bars

Boquitas Pintadas, Estados Unidos 1393 (Constitución), T4381 6064. Trendy pop-style bar holding art exhibitions.

Buller Brewing Company, Roberto M Ortiz 1827 (Recoleta). Brew pub. Happy hour till 2100.

La Cigale, 25 de Mayo 722, T4312 8275. Popular after office hours, good music, guest DJs on Tue.

The corner of Reconquista and Marcelo T de Alvear in Retiro is the centre of the small 'Irish' pub district, overcrowded on St Patrick's Day, 17 Mar. **Druid In**, Reconquista 1040, is by far the most attractive choice there, open for lunch and with live music weekly. **The Shamrock**, Rodríguez Peña 1220. Irish-run, popular, happy hour 1800-2400, Sat-Sun from 2000. Rock and electronic music in the basement.

There are good bars in San Telmo around Plaza Dorrego.

In Palermo Viejo, live music usually begins 2330-2400. Las Cañitas is best on Thu night; not so appealing at weekends. Good and popular are: **Bar 6**, Armenia 1676, T4833 6807, chic modern bar, good lunches, friendly atmosphere. **Mundo Bizarro**, Serrano 1222, famous for its cocktails, American-style food, electronic and pop music.

Clubs
El Living, M T de Alvear 1540, T4811 4730, www.living.com.ar. Relaxed bar, restaurant and small club, Thu-Sat.
Maluco Beleza, Sarmiento 1728. Brazilian flavour, entertaining, popular.
Niceto Club, Niceto Vega 5510, T4779 9396, www.nicetoclub.com. Early live shows and funk or electronic music for dancing afterwards.
Pacha, Av Costanera Rafael Obligado y Pampa, T4788 4280, www.pachabuenos aires.com. Electronic music on Sat.
The Roxy, Federico Lacroze y Álvarez Thomas. Rock, pop and live shows, Sat-Sun.

Gay clubs Most gay clubs charge US$10 entry. **Amerika**, Gascón 1040, www.ameri-k.com.ar. Thu-Sun. **Glam**, Cabrera 3046, www.glambsas.com.ar. Thu and Sat. **Alsina**, Alsina 940, www.alsina buenosaires.com.ar. Fri and Sun.
Sitges, Av Córdoba 4119, T4861 2763, www.sitgesonline.com.ar. Gay and lesbian bar, near Amerika.

Jazz clubs **Notorious**, Av Callao 966, T4813 6888, www.notorious.com.ar. Live jazz at a music shop. **La Revuelta**, Alvarez

Thomas 1368, T4553 5530. Live jazz, bossa nova and tango. **Thelonious**, Salguero 1884, T4829 1562. Live jazz and tango.
Salsa clubs La Salsera, Yatay 961, T4864 1733, www.lasalsera.com. Highly regarded.

⊕ Entertainment

Details of most events are given in Espectáculos/Entretenimientos section of main newspapers, *Buenos Aires Herald* (English) on Fri and www.whatsupbuenosaires.com.

Cinemas
The selection of films is excellent, ranging from new Hollywood releases to Argentine and world cinema; details are listed daily in main newspapers. Films are shown uncensored and most foreign films are subtitled. Tickets best booked early afternoon to ensure good seats (average price US$4, discount on Wed and for first show daily). Tickets obtainable from ticket agencies (*carteleras*), such as **Vea Más**, Paseo La Plaza, Corrientes 1660, local 2, T6320 5302 (the cheapest), **Cartelera**, Lavalle 742, T4322 1559, **Cartelera Baires**, Corrientes 1382, local 24, T4372 5058, www.cartelera-net.com.ar, and **Entradas con Descuento**, Lavalle 835, local 27, T4322 9263.

Seats can be booked by phone with credit/debit card for US$0.30 per ticket. Many cinemas in shopping malls, some on Av Corrientes and on C Lavalle, also in Puerto Madero (Dock 1) and in Belgrano (Av Cabildo). On Fri and Sat many central cinemas have *trasnoches*, late shows at 0100. At **Village Recoleta** (Vicente López y Junín) there is a cinema complex with *trasnoche* programmes on Fri and Sat. Independent foreign and national films are shown during the **Festival de Cine Independiente**, held every Apr, more information on the festival at www.bafici.gov.ar.

Cultural events

Centro Cultural Borges, Galerías Pacífico, Viamonte y San Martín, p 1, T5555 5359, www.ccborges.org.ar. Art exhibitions, concerts, film shows and ballet; some student discounts.

Centro Cultural Recoleta, Junín 1930, by Recoleta cemetery. Many free activities (see under Sights).

Ciudad Cultural Konex, Sarmiento 3131 (Abasto), T4864 3200, www.ciudadcultural konex.org. A converted oil factory hosts this huge complex holding plays, live music shows, summer film projections under the stars, modern ballet, puppet theatre and, occasionally, massive parties.

Fundación Proa, Av Pedro de Mendoza 1929, T4303 0909, www.proa.org. Temporary exhibitions of contemporary art, photography and other cultural events in La Boca.

Luna Park stadium, Bouchard 465, near Correo Central, T5279 5279, www.lunapark.com.ar. Pop/jazz concerts, sports events, ballet and musicals.

Museo de Arte Latinoamericano, MALBA, (address and website above), is a very active centre holding old or independent film exhibitions, seminars and conferences on arts.

Palais de Glace, Posadas 1725, T4804 1163, www.palaisdeglace.org. Temporary art and film exhibitions and other cultural events.

Teatro Gral San Martín, Corrientes 1530, T4371 0111/8, www.teatrosan martin.com.ar. Cultural activities, many free, including concerts, 50% ISIC discount for Thu, Fri and Sun (only in advance at 4th floor, Mon-Fri). The theatre's **Sala Leopoldo Lugones** shows international classic films, US$2.50.

Tango shows

Tango shows are mostly overpriced and tourist-oriented. Despite this, the music and dance are generally of a high professional standard and the shows very entertaining. Tango information office at Av Roque Sáenz Peña (Diagonal Norte) 832 p 6, T4393 4670,
www.tangodata.com.ar. Also www.tango city.com and www.todotango. com.

Every year, between end Feb-Mar the city celebrates the **Festival Buenos Aires Tango**, holding tango sessions, lessons, old musical films, exhibitions and a massive open-air *milonga*, open to all, in the central avenues (www.tangodata.gov.ar for details). Every August there is a tango dancing competition open to both locals and foreigners.

Bar Sur, Estados Unidos 299, T4362 6086, www.bar-sur.com.ar. 2000-0200, US$50; plus dinner for US$70 including pizza, tapas and empanadas, drinks extra. Good fun, public sometimes join the professional dancers.

El Querandí, Perú 302, T5199 1771, www.querandi.com.ar. Tango show restaurant, daily show (2200) US$56 dinner including drink (2030), and show US$80.

El Viejo Almacén, Independencia y Balcarce, T4307 7388, www.viejoalmacen.com. Daily, dinner from 2000, show 2200, US$80 with all drinks, dinner and show; show only, US$55. Impressive dancing and singing, recommended.

Esquina Carlos Gardel, Carlos Gardel 3200 y Anchorena, T4867 6363, www.esquinacarlos gardel.com.ar. Opposite the former Mercado del Abasto, this is the most popular venue in Gardel's own neighbourhood; dinner at 2030 (dinner and show US$83), show at 2230 (US$56). Recommended.

La Ventana, Balcarce 431, T4334 1314, www.la-ventana.com.ar. Daily dinner from 2000 (dinner and show US$80) or show with 2 drinks, 2200, US$57, very touristy but very good.

Piazzolla Tango, Florida 165 (basement), Galería Güemes, T4344 8200, www.piazzolla tango.com. A beautifully restored belle époque hall hosts a smart tango show; dinner at 2045 (dinner and show US$80), show at 2215 (US$60).

Señor Tango, Vieytes 1655, Barracas, T4303 0231, www.senortango.com.ar. Spectacular show with dancers, horses, etc, US$27, starts 2200 (with dinner at 2030, US$80).

Milongas are the events where locals dance tango and also *milonga* (the music that contributed to the origins of tango and is more cheerful). Tourists may join the dancers, or just watch (entry fee is much cheaper than for the shows); dancing is usually preceded by tango lessons. Milongas take place at several locations on different days; phone to confirm or check at www.tangodata.com.ar.

Centro Cultural Torquato Tasso, Defensa 1575, T4307 6506, www.torquatotasso. com.ar. Tue and Sun 2130, free (daily lessons 1700, 1830, US$5), English spoken.

Confitería Ideal, Suipacha 384, T5265 8069, www.confiteriaideal.com. Very atmospheric ballroom for daily milongas at this old central café. Most days dancing starts as early as 1500; lessons Mon-Fri start at 1200, Sat 2100. Also evening tango shows.

La Viruta (at Centro Armenio), Armenia 1366, Palermo Viejo, T4774 6357, www.la virutatango. com. Very popular with a young and trendy crowd, Wed-Sun (check for times).

Porteño y Bailarín, Riobamba 345, T4932 5452, www.porteybailarin.com.ar. Lessons Tue, Sun at 2100, dancing at 2300.

Tango Discovery, www.tangodiscovery.com. Offers unconventional method for tango lessons developed by dancer Mauricio Castro.

Theatre
You are advised to book as early as possible for a seat at a concert, ballet, or opera. Tickets for most popular shows (including rock and pop concerts) are sold also through **Ticketek**, T5237 7200, www.ticketek.com.ar, **Entrada Plus**, T4000 1010, www.entradaplus.com.ar, or **Ticketmaster**, T4321 9700. For other ticket agencies, see Cinemas, above. The **Teatro Colón**'s opera season usually runs from Apr to Nov and there are concert performances most days. Visit www.teatro colon.org.ar for news as redevolopment of the theatre is expected to be completed in 2010. For live Argentine and Latinamerican bands, best

venues are: **La Trastienda**, www.latrastienda. com, **ND Ateneo**, www.ndateneo.com.ar or **La Peña del Colorado**, www.delcolorado.com.ar.

○ Shopping

Most shops outside main shopping areas and malls close lunchtime on Sat. The main, fashionable shopping streets are Florida and Santa Fe (especially between 1000 and 2000 blocks). Palermo is the best area for chic boutiques and well-known international fashion labels. C Defensa in San Telmo is known for its antique shops. Pasaje de la Defensa, Defensa 1179, is a beautifully restored 1880s house containing small shops.

Bookshops
You'll find most bookshops along Florida, Av Corrientes (from Av 9 de Julio to Callao) or Av Santa Fe, and in shopping malls. Second-hand and discount bookshops are mostly along Av Corrientes and Av de Mayo. Rare books are sold in several specialized stores in the Microcentro (the area enclosed by Suipacha, Esmeralda, Tucumán and Paraguay). The main chains of bookshops, usually selling a small selection of foreign books, are: **Cúspide**, with several branches on Florida, Av Corrientes and some malls, and the biggest and most interesting store at Village Recoleta, Vicente López y Junín; **Distal**, Florida 738 and more branches on Florida and Av Corrientes; **El Ateneo**, whose biggest store is on Av Santa Fe 1860, in an old theatre, there is café where the stage used to be; **Yenny** in all shopping malls, also sell music. The **Boutique del Libro** chain is also good, the nicest branch being in Palermo, Thames 1762, T4833 6637, with a café, www.boutiquedellibro.com.ar. For a larger selection of books in English: **Crack Up**, Costa Rica 4767, T4831 3502. Funky, open plan bookshop and café, open Mon-Wed till 2230, and till the early hrs the rest of the week. **Eterna Cadencia**, Honduras 5574, T4774 4100. Excellent selection of novels,

classics, contemporary fiction and translations of Spanish and Argentine authors. Highly recommended for its café too. **Walrus Books**, Estados Unidos 617, San Telmo, www.walrus-books.com.ar. Second-hand books in English, including Latin American authors. Good children's section.

You can also try **ABC**, Maipú 866; **Joyce, Proust & Co**, Tucumán 1545 p 1 A, also sells books in other European languages; **Kel**, Marcelo T de Alvear 1369; **Librería Rodríguez**, Sarmiento 835; **LOLA**, Viamonte 976, Mon-Fri 1200-1830, small publishers specializing in Latin America natural history, also sell used and rare editions, most in English.

Foreign newspapers are available from news-stands on Florida, in Recoleta and the kiosk at Corrientes and Maipú.

Handicrafts

Alhué, Juncal 1625. Very good aboriginal-style crafts. **Arte y Esperanza**, Balcarce 234, www.arteyesperanza.com.ar. Crafts made by aboriginal communities, sold by a Fair Trade organization. **Artesanías Argentinas**, Montevideo 1386, www.artesaniasargentinas. org. Aboriginal crafts and other traditional items sold by a Fair Trade organization. **Atípica**, El Salvador 4510, Palermo Viejo, T4833 3344, www.atipicaobjetos.com.ar. Specializing in arts and crafts by local artists and designers, English, French and Portuguese spoken, see also Nancy Kulfas' trendypalermoviejo. blogspot.com. **Casa de San Antonio de los Cobres**, Pasaje de la Defensa, Defensa 1179, www.vivirenlos cobres.com.ar. Traditional Puna crafts in silver, llama or sheep wool. **El Boyero**, Florida 953, T4312 3564. High quality silver, leather, woodwork and other typical Argentine handicrafts. **Martín Fierro**, Santa Fe 992. Good handicrafts, stonework, etc. Recommended. **Plata Nativa**, Galería del Sol, Florida 860, local 41. For Latin American folk handicrafts and high quality jewellery.

Leather goods

Several shops are concentrated along Florida next to Plaza San Martín and also in Suipacha (900 block). **Aida**, Galería de la Flor, local 30, Florida 670. Quality, inexpensive leather products, can make a leather jacket to measure in the same day. **All Horses**, Suipacha 1350. Quality leather clothing. **Dalla Fontana**, Reconquista 735. Leather factory, fast, efficient and reasonably priced for made-to-measure clothes. **Casa López**, MT de Alvear 640/658; also at Patio Bullrich and Galerías Pacífico malls. The most traditional and finest leather shop, expensive but worth it. **Fortín**, Santa Fe 1245. Excellent items. **Galería del Caminante**, Florida 844. Has a variety of good shops with leather goods, arts and crafts, souvenirs, etc. **King's Game**, Maipú 984. Another good shop focusing on polo clothing. **La Curtiembre**, Juncal 1173, Paraguay 670. Affordable prices for good quality articles. **Prüne**, Florida 963 and at Florida y Av Córdoba. Fashionable designs for women, many options in leather and not very expensive. **Uma**, in shopping malls and at Honduras 5225 (Palermo Viejo). For women, the trendiest of all.

Markets

Caminito, Vuelta de Rocha (Boca), 1000-1700. Plastic arts and local crafts. **Costanera Sur**, next to the Fuente de las Nereidas. Weekends 1100-2000. Crafts, books, coins, stamps. **Feria Hippie**, in Recoleta, near cemetery. Big craft and jewellery market, Sat and Sun 1000-2200, good street atmosphere, expensive. **Feria de Mataderos**, Lisandro de la Torre y Av de los Corrales 6436, T4687 1949, subte E to end of line then taxi (US$3.50), or buses 36, 92, 97, 126, 141. Long way but few tourists, fair of Argentine handicrafts and traditions, music and dance festivals, gaucho horsemanship skills, every Sun 1200-1800 (Sat 1800-2400 in summer); nearby *Museo de los Corrales*, Av de los Corrales 6436,

T4687 1949, Sun 1200-1800 (in summer, Sat 1800-2300), US$0.35. **Mercado de las Luces**, Manzana de las Luces, Perú y Alsina, Mon-Fri 1100-1900, Sun 1400-1900. Handicrafts, second-hand books, plastic arts. **Parque Centenario**, Díaz Vélez y L Marechal. Sat-Sun 1100-2000, local crafts, cheap handmade clothes, used items of all sorts. **Parque Lezama**, Brasil y Defensa, San Telmo. Handicraft market at weekends, 1100-2000. **Parque Rivadavia**, Av Rivadavia 4900. Second-hand books, records, tapes, CDs and magazines (daily); **Feria del Ombú**, for stamps, postcards and coins (Sun 0930-1430, under a big ombú tree). **Plaza Belgrano**, near Belgrano Barrancas station on Juramento, between Cuba y Obligado. Sat-Sun, 1100-2000 craft, jewellery, etc market. **Plaza Dorrego**, San Telmo. For souvenirs, antiques, etc, with free tango performances and live music, Sun 1000-1700, wonderfully atmospheric, and an array of 'antiques'. **Plaza Italia**, Santa Fe y Uriarte (Palermo). Second-hand textbooks and magazines (daily), handicrafts market on Sat-Sun 1100-2000.

Music shops

Casa Piscitelli, San Martín 450. Classical, tango, folklore, jazz.
Zival's, Av Corrientes y Av Callao. Huge choice; also bookshop.

Shopping malls

Abasto de Buenos Aires, Av Corrientes 3247, T4959 3400, nearest Subte: Carlos Gardel, line B. In the city's impressive, Art Deco former fruit and vegetable market building: cheaper clothes, good choice, cinemas. **Alto Palermo**, Col Díaz y Santa Fe, T5777 8000, nearest Subte: opposite Bulnes, line D. Great for all the main clothes chain stores, and about 20 blocks' walk from Palermo's boutiques. **Galerías Pacífico**, on Florida, between Córdoba and Viamonte, T5555 5110, nearest Subte: Plaza San Martín, line C. A beautiful

mall with fine murals and architecture, many exclusive shops and good food mall with wide choice and low prices in basement. Also good set-price restaurant on 2nd floor (lunches only). Free guided visits from the fountain on lower-ground floor (Mon-Fri 1130, 1630). **Paseo Alcorta**, Salguero y Figueroa Alcorta, T5777 6500. Huge mall, spanning four levels, with cinemas, supermarket, stores, many cheap restaurants (take colectivo 130 from Retiro or Correo Central, or 67 from Constitución or Recoleta). **Patio Bullrich**, Av Del Libertador 750 and Posadas 1245, T4814 7400, nearest Subte: 8 blocks from Plaza San Martín, line C. The most upmarket mall in the city, selling chic international and Argentine fashion designer clothes, boutiques selling high-quality leather goods, and small food court in elegant surroundings.

▲ Activities and tours

Football and rugby Football fans should see **Boca Juniors**, matches every other Sun 1500-1900 at their stadium (La Bombonera, Brandsen 805, La Boca, www.bocajuniors. com.ar, tickets for non-members only through tour operators, or the museum, T4362 1100 – see the murals; along Av Almirante Brown buses 29, 33, 53, 64, 86, 152, 168; along Av Patricios buses 10, 22, 39, 93), or their arch-rivals, **River Plate**, www.cariver plate.com.ar (to stadium take bus 29, 130 from centre going north, or bus 15 from Palermo). Football season mid-Feb to Jun, and Aug-Dec, most matches on Sun and sometimes Fri or Sat (occasionally Tue-Thu). Buy tickets (from US$8) from stadiums, sports stores near the grounds, ticket agencies such as Ticketek or hostels and hotels, which may arrange guide/transport (don't take a bus if traveling alone, phone a radio taxi; see also Tangol, below). Rugby season Apr-Oct/Nov. For more information, **Unión Argentina de Rugby**, T4383 2211, www.uar.com.ar.

Tour operators and travel agents

An excellent way of seeing Buenos Aires and the surrounding area is by a 3-hr tour. Longer tours include dinner and a tango show, or a gaucho *fiesta* at a ranch (great food and dancing). Bookable through most travel agents.

Barba Charters, T4824 3366, www.barba charters.com.ar. Boat trips and fishing in the Delta and Tigre areas.

BAT, Buenos Aires Tur, Lavalle 1444 of 10, T4371 2304, www.buenosairestur.com. City tours, US$13, twice daily; Tigre and Delta, daily, 5 hrs, US$23.

Buenos Aires Vision, Esmeralda 356, p 8, T4394 4682, www.buenosaires-vision.com.ar. City tours (US$13), Tigre and Delta (from US$23), Tango (US$80-100, cheaper without dinner) and *Fiesta Gaucha* (US$55).

Cicerones de Buenos Aires, J J Biedma 883, T4330 0800, www.cicerones.org.ar. Non-profit organization offering volunteer "greeting"/ guiding service for visitors to the city; free, safe and a different experience.

Cultour, T156-365 6892 (mob), www.cultour. com.ar. A highly recommended walking tour of the city, 3-4 hrs led by a group of Argentine history/ tourism graduates, US$18. In English and Spanish.

Ecole del Sur, Av Rivadavia 1479, p 1 B, T4383 1026, www.ecoledelsur.com. Tour operator offering packages and accommodation in Buenos Aires, Argentina and Uruguay. Associated with **The Royal Family**, www.theroyalfamily.com.ar, gay and lesbian tourism and language school.

Eternautas, Av Julio A Roca 584 p 7, T5235 7295, www.eternautas.com. Historical, cultural and artistic tours of the city and Pampas guided in English, French or Spanish by academics from the University of Buenos Aires, flexible.

Eves Turismo, Tucumán 702, T4393 6151, www.eves.com. Helpful and efficient, recommended for flights.

Flyer, Reconquista 617, p 8, T4313 8224, www.flyer.com.ar. English, Dutch, German spoken, repeatedly recommended, especially for *estancias*, fishing, polo, motorhome rental.

HI Travel Argentina, Florida 835, ground floor, T4511 8723, www.hitravel.com.ar.

Hostelling International Travel, Florida 835 PB, T4511 8723, www.hostels.org.ar. Hostel network office and advisors, specialised backpacker trips.

L'Open Tour, T4116 4544, www.lopen tour.com.ar. Multilingual, 2-hr recorded tours (headphones provided) on an open bus, leaving 4 times a day, either to the south or to the north, from Plaza San Martín (opposite **Marriott Hotel**), US$20. Book in advance.

Lan&Kramer Bike Tours, T4311 5199, www.bike tours.com.ar. Daily at 0930 and 1400 next to the monument of San Martín (Plaza San Martín), 3½-4-hr cycle tours to the south or the north of the city (US$30); they also go to San Isidro and Tigre, 4½-5 hrs, US$35, bike rental at Florida 868, p 14H.

Nomads Community Travel Agency, Lima 11, T5218 3059. Offers flight and bus tickets, specialized guides, various tours and activities and custom-made trips.

Patagonia Chopper, www.patagonia chopper.com.ar. Helicopter tours of Buenos Aires and around,15-45 mins, US$165-248 pp (min 2 people; price includes transfer in/ out to/from the city centre). Flights also to Colonia and the Delta.

Pride Travel, Paraguay 523 p 2, T5218 6556, www.pride-travel.com. For gay and lesbian travellers; also rents apartments and also at Guatemala 4845, p 1 of 4, Palermo.

Say Hueque, Viamonte 749, p 6 of 1, T5199 2517/ 20, www.sayhueque.com. Recommended travel agency offering good-value tours aimed at independent travellers, friendly English-speaking staff. Specialize in tours to Patagonia, Iguazu and Mendoza.

Smile on Sea, T15-5018 8662 (mob), www.smileonsea.com. 2½-hr private boat trips off Buenos Aires coast, leaving from Puerto Madero, on 32-ft sailing boats

(US$242 for up to 5 passengers). Also 8-hr trips to San Isidro and Delta (US$600 for 5).

Tangol, Florida 971, ground floor, shop 31, T4312 7276, www.tangol.com. Friendly, independent agency specializing in football and tango, plus various sports, such as polo and paragliding. Can arrange tours, plane and bus tickets, accommodation. English spoken. Discounts for students. Overland tours in Patagonia Sep-Apr.

Urban biking, Moliere 2801 (Villa Devoto), T4568 4321, www.urbanbiking.com. 4½-hr tours either to the south or to the north of the centre, starting daily 0900 and 1400 next to the English clock tower in Retiro, US$24. Night city tours, 3½ hrs, US$28, full day tours to San Isidro and Tigre (including kayak in the Delta), US$50, or occasionally, to the pampas. Also rents bikes.

What's Up BA, T4553 8827, http://whatsup buenosaires.com. For a wide variety of cultural experiences around the city, including finding accommodation.

⊖ Transport

Air

Ezeiza (officially Ministro Pistarini, T5480 6111, www.aa2000.com.ar), the international airport, is 35 km southwest of the centre (also handles some domestic flights to El Calafate and Ushuaia in high season). The airport has 2 terminals: 'A' for all airlines except **Aerolíneas Argentinas**, which uses 'B'. 'A' has a very modern check-in hall. There are duty free shops (expensive), exchange facilities (**Banco de la Nación; Banco Piano; Global Exchange** – rates of exchange in baggage reclaim are considerably poorer than elsewhere – only change the minimum to get you into the city) and ATMs (Visa and MasterCard), a Secretaría de Turismo desk, post office (open 0800-2000) and a left luggage office (US$3 per piece). No hotels nearby, but there is an attractive B&B 5 mins away with transfer included: **$$$ Bernie's**, Estrada 186, Barrio Esteban Echeverría, T4480

0420, www.posada bernies.com.ar, book in advance. There is a **Devolución IVA/Tax Free** desk (return of VAT) for purchases over the value of AR$70 (ask for a Global Refund check plus the invoice from the shop when you buy). Reports of pilfering from luggage. To discourage this have your bags sealed by Secure Bag in the check-in hall. Hotel booking service at Tourist Information desk – helpful, but prices are higher if booked in this way. A display in immigration shows choices and prices of transport into the city.

Airport buses Special buses to/from the centre are run by **Manuel Tienda León** (office in front of you as you arrive), company office and terminal at Av Madero 1299 y San Martín, behind Sheraton Hotel in Retiro, T4315 5115, www.tiendaleon.com. To **Ezeiza**: 0400, 0500, then every 30 mins till 2100 and 2200, 2230, 2400 (be 15 mins early); from Ezeiza: more-or-less hourly throughout the day and night, US$11.50 (US$21.50 return), 40-min journey, pay by pesos, dollars, euros or credit card. **Manuel Tienda León** will also collect passengers from addresses in centre for US$1 extra, book the previous day. Bus from Ezeiza to Aeroparque, 1 hr, US$12. Remise taxis to town or to Aeroparque, US$38. Services on request with **Transfer Express**, T0800-444 4872, reservas@transfer-express.com.ar, airport office in front of you as you arrive, remise taxi from Ezeiza to town or to Aeroparque, US$30. **Taxi Ezeiza**, T5480 0066, www.taxiezeiza.com.ar, US$30 to the centre, US$35 to Aeroparque. Also **VIP** and **World Car** with similar prices.

Aeroparque (Jorge Newbery Airport), 4 km north of the centre, TT5480 6111, www.aa2000.com.ar, handles all internal flights, and **AR** and **Pluna** flights to Montevideo and Punta del Este. The terminal is divided into 2 sections, 'A' for all arrivals and **AR/Austral** and **LAN** check-in desks, 'B' for **Pluna**, **Andes**, **Sol** and **LADE** check-in desks. On the 1st floor there is a **patio de comidas** and many shops. At the airport also tourist information, car rental, bus companies, bank, ATMs, exchange facilities, post office, public phones, Secure Bag (US$8 per piece) and luggage deposit (between sections A-B at the information point), US$2 per piece for 12 hrs. **Manuel Tienda León** buses to Aeroparque (see above for address), 0710-0040, every hour; from Aeroparque (departs from sector B, stops at **AR**), 0900-1600 every hour, and 1800, 2000, 2130 and 2330, 20-min journey, US$4. Local buses 33 and 45 run from outside the airport to the Retiro railway station, then to **La Boca** and **Constitución** respectively. No 37 goes to **Palermo** and **Recoleta** and No 160 to **Palermo** and **Almagro**. If going to the airport, make sure it goes to Aeroparque by asking the driver, US$0.33. **Remise taxis**: are operated by **Transfer Express** and **Manuel Tienda León**, US$8-9 to centre, US$38 to Ezeiza. Taxi to centre US$6. **Manuel Tienda León** operates buses between Ezeiza and Aeroparque airports, US$12, stopping in city centre, US$4. **AR/Austral** offer daily flights to the main cities; **LAN** has daily flights to some cities and tourist destinations; **Andes** flies to Salta and to Puerto Madryn, **Sol** flies to Rosario, Santa Fe and Córdoba (and in summer to Mar del Plata, Villa Gesell, Montevideo and Punta del Este), for details see text under intended destination. **LADE** offers weekly flights to **El Calafate, Ushuaia, Puerto Madryn** and **Bariloche** with several stops in Patagonia.

Bus

Local City buses are called *colectivos* and cover a very wide radius. They are clean, frequent, efficient and very fast. The basic fare is about US$0.30, US$0.50 to the suburbs. Have coins ready for ticket machine as drivers do not sell tickets, but may give change. The bus number is not always sufficient indication of destination, as each number may have a variety of routes, but bus stops display routes of buses stopping there and little plaques are displayed in the driver's window. No 86

(white and blue) runs to the centre from outside the airport terminal to the left as you leave the building, 2 hrs, US$0.50, coins only, runs all day, every 20 mins during the day. To travel to Ezeiza, catch the bus at Av de Mayo y Perú, 1 block from Plaza de Mayo (many other stops, but this is central) – make sure it has 'Aeropuerto' red sign in the window as many 86s stop short of Ezeiza. See Ins and outs, above, for city guides listing bus routes.

International buses International services are run by both local and foreign companies; heavily booked Dec-Mar (especially at weekends), when most fares usually rise sharply; fares shown here are for high season. Do not buy Uruguayan bus tickets in Buenos Aires; wait till you get to Colonia. To **Montevideo** Bus de la Carrera, Mon, Wed, Fri 1000, US$27, 8 hrs, with a *coche cama*, daily at 2230, via Colón and Paysandú. CAUVI also goes daily to Montevideo at 2130, and in summer to **Punta del Este**.

Driving

Driving in Buenos Aires is no problem, provided you have eyes in the back of your head and good nerves. Traffic fines are high and police increasingly on the lookout for drivers without the correct papers. Car hire is cheaper if you arrange it when you arrive rather than from home. Also **Sixt**, Carlos Pellegrini 1537, T4328 8020, www.sixt.com.ar, and **Thrifty**, Carlos Pellegrini 1576, T0810-999 8500, www.thriftyar.com.ar. There are several national rental agencies, eg **Serra Lima**, Av Córdoba 3121, T4962 8508 or T0800-777 5462, or **Dietrich**, Cerrito 1575, T0810-345 3438, www.dietrich rentacar.com. **Ruta Sur**, Lavalle 482, p 5, T5238 4072, www.rutasur. com. Rents 4WDs and motorhomes.

Ferry

To **Montevideo** and **Colonia** from Terminal Dársena Norte, Av Antártida Argentina 821 (2 blocks from Av Córdoba y Alem). **Buquebus**, T4316 6400, www.buquebus.com

(tickets from Terminal or from offices at Av Córdoba 8/9 and Posadas 1452): 1) Direct to **Montevideo**, 2 a day, 3 hrs, US$69 tourist class, US$97 1st class, US$111 special class one way, vehicles US$86-112, motorcycles US$70, bus connection to Punta del Este, US$11 extra. 2) To **Colonia**, services by 2 companies: **Buquebus**: minimum 5 crossings a day, from 1 to 3 hrs, US$27 tourist class, US$37 1st class, US$44 special class one way, US$37-55 on fast vessels, with bus connection to **Montevideo** (US$11 extra). Motorcycles US$34-45, cars US$51-75 and 68-95 (depending on size of vehicle and boat). **Colonia Express**, www.coloniaexpress. com, makes 2-3 crossings a day between Buenos Aires and Colonia in a fast catamaran (no vehicles carried), 50 mins, prices start at US$6 one way if bought on the internet, or US$12 with bus connections to Montevideo; non-web prices are much higher, eg US$15-38 one way to Colonia, US$27-110 to Montevideo. Office is at Av Córdoba 753, T4313 5100; Terminal Fluvial is at Av Pedro de Mendoza 330, T4317 4100. You must go there by taxi. See under Tigre, page , for services to Carmelo and Nueva Palmira.

Metro (Subte)

Six lines link the outer parts of the city to the centre. **Line 'A'** runs under Av Rivadavia, from Plaza de Mayo to Primera Junta. **Line 'B'** from central Post Office, on Av L N Alem, under Av Corrientes to Federico Lacroze railway station at Chacarita, ending at Los Incas. **Line 'C'** links Plaza Constitución with the Retiro railway station, and provides connections with all the other lines but 'H'. **Line 'D'** runs from Plaza de Mayo (Catedral), under Av Roque Sáenz Peña (Diagonal Norte), Córdoba, Santa Fe and Palermo to Congreso de Tucumán (Belgrano). **Line 'E'** runs from Plaza de Mayo (Cabildo, on C Bolívar) through San Juan to Plaza de los Virreyes (connection to Premetro train service to the southwest end of the city). **Line 'H'** runs from Once to Caseros, under Av Jujuy.

Note that 3 stations, 9 de Julio (Line 'D'), Diagonal Norte (Line 'C') and Carlos Pellegrini (Line 'B') are linked by pedestrian tunnels. The fare is US$0.30, the same for any direct trip or combination between lines; magnetic cards (for 1, 2, 5, 10 or 30 journeys) must be bought at the station before boarding; only pesos accepted. Trains are operated by **Metrovías**, T0800-555 1616, and run Mon-Sat 0500-2225 (Sun 0800-2200). Line A, the oldest was built in 1913, the earliest in South America; it starts running Mon-Sat at 0600. Backpacks and luggage allowed. Free map (if available) from stations and tourist office.

Taxi

Taxis are painted yellow and black, and carry Taxi flags. Fares are shown in pesos. The meter starts at US$1 when the flag goes down; make sure it isn't running when you get in. A fixed rate of US$0.10 for every 200 m or 1-min wait is charged thereafter. A charge is sometimes made for each piece of hand baggage (ask first). About 10% tip expected. Phone a radio taxi from a phone box or locutorio, giving the address of where you are, and you'll usually be collected within 5 mins. Taxis from official rank in bus terminal are registered with police and safe. For extra security, take a remise taxi booked from a booth on the bus platform itself, more expensive but very secure (to Ezeiza US$26; to Aeroparque US$9). Taxis from a registered company are safer, and some 'Radio Taxis' you see on the street are false. Check that the driver's licence is displayed. Lock doors on the inside. Worst places are the 2 airports and Retiro; make sure you know roughly what the fare should be before the journey: eg from Aeroparque to: Ezeiza US$21 (plus toll), Congreso US$6, Plaza de Mayo US$6, Retiro US$5, La Boca US$8. In theory fares double for journeys outside city limits (Gen Paz circular highway), but you can often negotiate. Radio Taxis (same colours and fares) are managed by several different companies (eg **Del Plata**, T4504 7776; **Pídalo**, T4956 1200; **Llámenos**, T4556 6666) and are recommended as a safer alternative; minimum fare is US$2.50.

Remise taxis operate all over the city, run from an office and have no meter. The companies are identified by signs on the pavement. Fares, which are fixed and can be cheaper than regular taxis, start at US$2.55-3 and can be verified by phoning the office, and items left in the car can easily be reclaimed. **La Terminal**, T4312 0711 is recommended, particularly from Retiro bus station.

From centre to **Ezeiza** US$26-31. Fixed-price *remise taxis* for up to 4 passengers can be booked from the **Manuel Tienda León** or **Transfer Express** counter at Ezeiza, prices above. Avoid unmarked cars at Ezeiza no matter how attractive the fare may sound; drivers are adept at separating you from far more money than you can possibly owe them. Always ask to see the taxi driver's licence. If you take an ordinary taxi the Policía de Seguridad Aeroportuaria on duty notes down the car's licence and time of departure. There have been recent reports of taxi drivers taking Ezeiza airport-bound passengers to remote places, stealing all their luggage and leaving them there. If in doubt, take a *remise* or airport bus.

Tram
Old-fashioned street cars operate Mar-Nov on Sat and holidays 1600-1930 and Sun 1000-1300, 1600-1930 and Dec-Feb on Sat and holidays 1700-2030, Sun 1000-1300, 1700-2030, free, on a circular route along the streets of Caballito district, from C Emilio Mitre 500, Subte Primera Junta (Line A) or Emilio Mitre (Line E), no stops en route. Operated by **Asociación Amigos del Tranvía**, T4431 1073, www.tranvia.org.ar. There is a new tram that runs along Av Alicia Moreau de Justo (Puerto Madero), with terminals at Av Córdoba and at Av Independencia, US$0.35.

Train
There are 4 main terminals: 1) **Retiro** (3 lines: **Mitre**, **Belgrano** and **San Martín** in separate buildings). Mitre line (run by **TBA**, T4317 4407 or T0800-333 3822, www.tbanet.com.ar). Urban and suburban services include: **Belgrano**, **Mitre** (connection to Tren de la Costa, see below), **Olivos**, **San Isidro**, and **Tigre** (see below); long distance services to **Rosario Norte**, Mon-Fri 1840, 5 hrs, US$11.

2) **Constitución**, Roca line urban and suburban services to La Plata, Ezeiza, Ranelagh and Quilmes. Long distance services (run by **Ferrobaires**, T4304 0028, www.ferrobaires. gba.gov.ar): Bahía Blanca, 5 weekly, 12½ hrs, US$10-16, food mediocre; to Mar del Plata daily, 6-7 hrs, US$11-20; to Pinamar, 1-2 weekly, 6 hrs, US$11-15; to Miramar (one a day in summer only), 8 hrs, US$13-16; to Carmen de Patagones, 20 hrs, weekly, US$18-20; also to Bolívar and Daireaux.

3) **Federico Lacroze** Urquiza line and Metro headquarters (run by **Metrovías**, T0800-555 1616, www.metrovias.com.ar). Suburban services: to General Lemos. **Trenes Especiales Argentinos**, T4554 8018, www.trenesdellitoral. com.ar, runs twice a week a train to **Posadas**, minimum 26 hrs, US$21-75, from Lacroze via the towns along Río Uruguay.

4) **Once**: Sarmiento line (run by *TBA*, see above). Urban and suburban services include **Luján** (connection at Moreno), **Mercedes** and **Lobos**. A fast service runs Mon-Fri between Puerto Madero (station at Av Alicia Moreau de Justo y Perón) and Castelar. Long distance services to Lincoln and Pehuajó (see www.ferrobaires.gba. gov.ar). Tickets checked before boarding and on train and collected at the end of the journey; urban and suburban fares are charged according different sections of each line; fares vary depending on the company, cheapest is about US$0.22.

Banks ATMs are widespread for MasterCard or Visa (look for Link ATMs). The financial district lies within a small area north of Plaza de Mayo, between Rivadavia, 25 de Mayo, Av Corrientes and Florida. In non-central areas find banks/ATMs along the main avenues. Banks open Mon-Fri 1000-1500. Use credit or debit cards for withdrawing cash rather than carrying TCs. Most banks charge commission especially on TCs (as much as US$10). US dollar bills are often scanned electronically for forgeries, while TCs are sometimes very difficult to change and you may be asked for proof of purchase. Major credit cards usually accepted but check for surcharges. General MasterCard office at Perú 151, T4348 7000, www.mastercard. com/ar, open 0930-1800. Visa, Corrientes 1437 p 2, T4379 3400, www.visa.com.ar.

Internet Prices range from US$0.40 to US$1 per hr, shop around. Most *locutorios* (phone offices) have internet access.

Medical services Urgent medical service: for free municipal ambulance service to an emergency hospital department (day and night) **Casualty ward**, **Sala de guardia**, T107 or T4923 1051/58 (SAME). Inoculations: **Hospital Rivadavia**, Av Las Heras 2670, T4809 2000, Mon-Fri, 0700-1200 (bus 10, 37, 59, 60, 62, 92, 93 or 102 from Plaza Constitución), or **Dirección de Sanidad de Fronteras y Terminales de Transporte**, Ing Huergo 690, T4343 1190, Mon 1400-1500, Tue-Wed 1100-1200, Thu and Fri 1500-1600, bus 20 from Retiro, no appointment required (yellow fever only; take passport). If not provided, buy the vaccines in **Laboratorio Biol**, Uriburu 153, T4953 7215, or in larger chemists. Many chemists have signs indicating that they give injections. Any hospital with an infectology department will give hepatitis A. **Travel Medicine Service (Centros Médicos Stamboulian)**, 25 de Mayo 464, T4515 3000, French 3085, T5236 7772, also in Belgrano and Flores, www.viajeros. cei.com.ar. Private health advice for travellers and inoculations centre. Public Hospitals: **Hospital Argerich**, Almte Brown esq Pi y Margall 750, T4121 0700. **Hospital Juan A Fernández**, Cerviño y Bulnes, T4808 2600/2650, probably the best free medical attention in the city. **British Hospital**, Perdriel 74, T4309 6400, www.hospital britanico.org.ar. US$24 a visit. **German Hospital**, Av Pueyrredón 1640, between Beruti and Juncal, T4827 7000, www.hospitalale man.com.ar. Both have first-aid centres (*centros asistenciales*) as do other main hospitals. Dental treatment at Solís 2180, T4305 2530/ 2110. Excellent dental treatment centre at **Carroll Forest**, Vuelta de Obligado 1551 (Belgrano), T4781 9037, www.carroll-forest. com.ar. **Post offices** Correo Central, Correos Argentinos, Sarmiento y Alem, T4891 9191, www.correo argentino. com.ar, Mon-Fri, 0800-2000, Sat 1000-1300. *Poste Restante* (only to/ from national destinations) on ground floor (US$0.35 per letter). **Telephone** International and local calls, internet and fax from phone offices (*locutorios* or *telecentros*), manye city centre.

Contents

Footnotes

Index